THE DARK AND BRIGHT CONTINENT:

Africa In The Changing World

BY

RICHARD ONUKEGAM NWACHUKWU

Published By

GOOD HOPE ENTERPRISES, INC.

P. O. Box 2394

Dallas, Texas 75221-2394

U. S. A.

Copyright 1989 By
Richard Onukegam Nwachukwu
All Rights Reserved

This book, THE DARK AND BRIGHT CONTINENT: Africa in the Changing World, may not be reproduced in whole or in part, by mimeograph or any other means, without written permission from the author or the publisher.

Published By

GOOD HOPE ENTERPRISES, INC.
P. O. Box 2394
Dallas, Texas   75221-2394
U. S. A.

Distributed in Some African Countries By
GOOD HOPE ENTERPRISES & COMMUNICATIONS LTD.
P. O. Box 72818
Victoria Island, Lagos, Nigeria

Printed in the United States of America
Library of Congress Catalog Card Number
89-80209
ISBN 0-941823-01-6

Cover Artwork By Robert Esparza

Note: A Combination of American and Queen's English spellings are used in this book.

Dedicated to my children:

Joyce Ihesinachi, Uchenna Richmond and Ikechukwu Prosper;

As well as

All men (and women) of goodwill, such as Prof. Chinua Achebe, Barristers Gani Fawehinmi and Nelson Mandela

THE DARK & BRIGHT CONTINENT: AFRICA IN THE CHANGING WORLD

THE TABLE OF CONTENT

1. ABOUT THE AUTHOR................ viii
2. PREFACE........................... xii
3. THE RHYTHMS OF LIFE............... 19

PART 1

4. ANCIENT AFRICAN POLITICS & BELIEFS......................... 25

   (i) Polygamy & Self Sufficiency... 28

   (ii) Polygamy and Religion & Culture.................... 29

5. SLAVERY & COLONIZATION AT A GLANCE.......................... 48

6. POLITICAL INDEPENDENCE............ 61

   (i) List of African sovereign nations showing dates of their independence................. 69

   (ii) Map of Contemporary Africa, showing countries and Major Languages................ 73, 74

7. ECONOMIC INDEPENDENCE............. 87

PART 2

8. COUP D' ETAT IN AFRICA............123
   Nigeria...........................128
   Ghana.............................138
   Egypt.............................142
   Sudan.............................145
   Central African Republic..........148
   Benin Republic....................150
   Burundi...........................152
   Cameroun..........................154
   Chad..............................155
   Comoros...........................158
   People's Republic of Congo........160
   Equatorial Guinea.................162
   Guinea............................163
   Guinea Bissau.....................164
   Lesotho...........................164
   Madagascar........................166
   Mali..............................167
   Algeria...........................168
   Mauritania........................169
   Niger Republic....................171
   Rwanda............................173
   Seychelles........................174
   Libya.............................174
   Burkina Faso......................177
   Sierra Leone......................185
   Somalia...........................187
   Togo..............................190
   Uganda............................192
   Zaire.............................200

   Analysis of Coup d' etat
      in Africa......................207

PART 3

9. RIP VAN WINKLE AS AFRICA.......... 220
10. SUMMARY OF OAU CHARTER........... 222
11. AFRICA AND THE WORLD............. 229
12. FOREIGN MEDIA AND AFRICA......... 256
    A LETTER FROM TIME MAGAZINE....... 271
    A PHOTOGRAPH SHOWING A SEGMENT
    OF LAGOS, NIGERIA................. 274
13. EXOGENOUS USE OF AFRICANS........ 288
14. EDUCATION AND DEVELOPMENT........ 303
15. THE FUTURE OF AFRICA............. 322
16. SPECIAL ACKNOWLEDGEMENT.......... 342

* * *

* * *

THE DARK & BRIGHT CONTINENT:
AFRICA IN THE CHANGING WORLD

ABOUT THE AUTHOR

Richard Onukegam Nwachukwu, the Author of, THE AGONY: The Untold Tale of the Nigerian Society, hails from Umuduru Amiri, Oru Local Government Area, Imo State, Nigeria. The second of six children of Nze Wilfred Onyeadusi and Lolo Mgbaru Margaret Nwachukwu, he received his primary education from St. Gerald's Primary School (now Community Primary School) Umuduru (Amiri) and St. Paul Central School, Amiri. His first year of secondary school education was at former Obiako Memorial Secondary School, Oguta in 1971 before he transferred to Dick Tiger Memorial Secondary School, Amaigbo, Orlu, Imo State. He graduated in June 1975.

After graduation, he took a job as a teacher at Holy Saviours College (Secondary school), Isolo, Lagos in September 1975. After six months of teaching experience, he accepted a position as a clerical officer with the

Barclays Bank of Nigeria Ltd., (now Union Bank of Nigeria Ltd.) on April 6, 1976. He worked in various departments and positions there before he left in June 1979 for further studies in the United States of America.

Richard Nwachukwu received his Bachelor of Science degree in Economics (with the Highest Hono(u)rs) from Alabama A & M University on December 18, 1981. While a student, he was elected Editor-in-Chief of the student newspaper, The Maroon & White. He was the first foreign student to win such a vote of confidence among his peers since the institution came into existence in 1875.

As a student, he received many honours and scholastic awards, among which were Who's Who Among Students in American Universities & Colleges, Outstanding Leadership Award, Outstanding Editor-in-Chief Award, Alabama A & M University Scholastic Achievement Award, Scholarship Award by Delta Mu Delta National Hono(u)r Society in Business Administration in "recognition of superior scholarship, leadership, and continuing studies in Business Administration," to mention but a few. By virtue of his position as an elected officer, he was an Executive Member of the Student Government Association.

In June 1982, Nwachukwu moved from Alabama to Texas. He accepted a position as a Night Auditor at the West Group, Inc., The Adolphus Hotel Division. He later became the Audit Manager. While working as Auditor, he was given admission for graduate studies at East Texas State University, Commerce, Texas, in January 1983. He graduated with a Master of Business Administration (MBA), in December 1983. He was thereafter given an admission for Post-Master's Programme in Human Resource Development and Management. In 1986, he left the Adolphus Hotel to join Republic Bank Corporation, which is now NCNB Texas National Bank.

Richard O. Nwachukwu left his Post-Master's Programme after a couple of years in order to study law. He is pursuing the degree of Doctor of Jurisprudence. He remains a registered law student with the Committee of Bar Examiners of the State Bar of California.

Although Richard Nwachukwu was still employed at NCNB Texas, he founded Good Hope Enterprises, Inc. He remains the Chairman of the Board. He is a member of various professional and social organizations, among which are American Institute of Bankers, International Association of Independent Publishers (COSMEP), to mention but a few.

As we prepared for the press, Nwachukwu was notified from Washington, D.C. about his nomination as Who's Who of

Nigerians in North America. He is
married with three children.

PUBLISHER
* * *

PREFACE

As my first book titled THE AGONY: The Untold Tale of the Nigerian Society was published in 1987, I considered relaxing for a while. But that would never happen. As I pondered the agony I went through in order to bring out what some called an "explosive" book, one of its admirers, Alvan Nwoke called me. He was impressed, not only with the polished English tailoring of the work, but also the fearless manner and the frankness of the content. He urged me to write a similar book about Africa. ("The Agony" can now be purchased directly from the Publisher - Good Hope Enterprises, Inc.)

My reply that what I had written about Nigeria, even though it centred on Patriotism, Bribery and Corruption, Nigerian Government and Foreign Multi-National Companies, Voodooism, Tribalism/Nepotism, The Nigerian Economy, Technological Stagnation, Human Relations, and The Nigerian Leadership, also reflect Africa in general, however, did not satisfy his curiosity. In fact, he started suggesting not only the title to the proposed book, but the likely content. My eventual reply to him, in order to let me alone, was "I would think about it."

As I was thinking about it, I started to reflect on the title he suggested: A Dark Continent. That sent me to the drawing board to conjugate not only the eventual title, but what might reflect my kind of philosophical writing. My first book had already earned me the title of "A Philosopher" by many readers. I would not let them down. Hence, the birth of the present title and the content of this book.

The writing of this book took me more time than I earlier envisioned. As I conducted the research, I was drawn into new discoveries and some "current" evolving issues extending beyond African Continent.

For the reader's convenience, I separated the book into three segments: Part one deals with Ancient African Politics and Beliefs, Slavery and Colonization (at a Glance), Political Independence, and Economic Independence; Part two deals with Coup D' Etat In Africa; and Part three contains Rip Van Winkle As Africa, the Summary of OAU Charter, Africa and the World, Foreign Media and Africa, Exogenous Use of Africans, Education and Development, and The Future of Africa.

Part two is the heart of this work. It deals exclusively with the Coup D' Etat in Africa. Only a handful of African nations have not suffered the wrath of a coup.

This book, again, is about change. Change is one of the characteristics of the evolution of life. Those who do not change are left behind and subdued. That is the fate Africa is left with. Tomorrow, as we ought to know, is for those who prepare for it today.

My research led me into making use of (the work of) various books, magazines and newspapers as shown by the special acknowledgement in this book. But in addition to that, I must extend my appreciation to the Dallas Times Herald, Dallas Morning News, Los Angeles Times, New York Times, Wall Street Journal, New York News Service, Washington Post, Business Week, Newsweek (all of U.S.A.); Newswatch, African Concord, and African Guardian (all of Nigeria) for the invaluable help I got from them. Their materials helped me in many ways to strengthen my points on various issues.

There were a lot of individuals who helped me in various ways to make this book a success. My thanks first of all goes to Alvan Nwoke who insisted that I put everything else aside and address the African situation. I must also thank Dan Agbese, Deputy Editor-in-Chief of Newswatch Magazine and Deputy Chief Executive Officer of Newswatch Communications (Nigeria) Ltd. for permitting me to make use of his works, particularly his Rhythms of Life. His permission without hesitation whatsoever, was noble and highly appreciated.

No book makes interesting reading without review and/or critique by some learned peers. John Ilokwu, an Executive Vice President of Total Utilities, Inc., and a doctoral student at the University of Texas at Dallas, spared time out of his busy schedule to review this book. Prof. Alphine Jefferson, The Director of African-American Studies at the Southern Methodist University (SMU) in Dallas, Texas, equally gave in his valuable time to review and critique the materials that became this book. E. Jack Morone, a colleague, helped me in his own way, and was sometimes indispensable in some brain-storm discussions during the early stage of this book. To these gentlemen I am highly indebted.

I was a full time employee at the NCNB Texas National Bank (formerly First Republic BankCorp.), Treasury Division, at the time I was writing this book. The high level of professionalism exercised by my co-workers, particularly Kindra L. Robinson, Kathleen M. Reilly, F. Mike Clarkson, Randy Levy, Mike Tassell, Tom Sadler, Randy White, Jacob Ray, Brent Andersen and Ron Kirkland was highly appreciated.

Other co-workers at the department

that made things bearable to some degree, and perhaps enthusiastic about this book include Nadine Waites, Patricia Maggi, Pinakin J. Jani, Rob Nelson, David Parrott, Gregory Gorman, Connie Cross, David Mann, Joanne Deboer, Grace Tang, Jacquie Brawner, Alexander De La Garza, Bruce Dunai, and Sherril English. To all of them, I say thanks.

There are a host of others who may have helped me during the course of writing this book whose names I must have certainly missed. I salute them all. However, I must not forget to mention Danny Miller, Tyron Wilson, and Frederick Bjorck (who in mid-1970s worked in Nigeria). Their encouraging words and brotherly advice were, and still are always appreciated.

Other persons that deserve many thanks are Holli Ball at the Bank's Public Affairs Dept., whose previous help was invaluable, Edward Adesodun at the Credit Card Dept., Robert Esparza, the artist of my two books, Anthony Ike Akabue, and Prof. Bernice Richardson of Alabama A&M University. To them, I am sincerely indebted.

I am personally responsible for the content of this book. It is possible that I may have inadvertently offended some interest groups or individuals, some who may even be my friends, during the analysis of some segments in this book.

Such incidents are bound to happen when writing a book of this nature. It is not by any means designed that way.

I do not claim that this is all there is about the situation in Africa. Of course, there could be more written, particularly as the world (now) "turns". But those are not the main objective of this book. This book is written to highlight the major African problems, how foreign media treat Africa, and the developed world's manipulation of Africans.

All criticism and complaints about this book should be directed to me. I welcome them.

My family was an integral part of the writing of this book. My wife Victoria who was not only caring about my son Uchenna, but also expecting our third child, Ikechukwu (born on January 4, 1989) typed the manuscript that became this book. My brother Hyginus Ubakananwa Nwachukwu who was my other arm in a distant country - Nigeria - helped to provide any necessary materials that I needed for the successful completion of this book. I am highly indebted to them.

My children who wanted to be on my arms during the course of writing this book were sometimes denied those rights due to the exigencies of writing a book of this nature. As a result of their

-xviiunputrefied sacrifice and the burden awaiting all children, particularly their generation that must right the wrongs of the present corrupt, inept politicians and military men in the developing countries, to them, along with all men of goodwill, such as Professor Chinua Achebe, Barrister Abdul Ganiyu Oyesola Fawehinmi, all of Nigeria, and Barrister Nelson Mandela of South Africa, this book is dedicated.

      Richard Onukegam Nwachukwu
        Dallas, Texas, USA

          * * *

* * *

RHYTHMS OF LIFE

With all its imperfections, life remains a reasonably well thought-out drama. Everyone has a part to play in it -- be it a leading part or a minor part. The different roles are the stuff of life's rhythm: the pluck on the guitar strings, drumsticks on the xylophone. Notice the melody, that tang which makes life so sweet, so desirable, yet often such a glorious waste.

It is a settled convention of life's drama that no man or woman be allowed on the stage for ever, partly because life for anyone does not go on forever and partly because life is a continuum with a capacity for self-renewal. Each man or woman is given a time, a period and a stage to act his part and depart. Some, to take their seat among the audience once again; others fade out and become part of the evolutionary process, to be remembered or forgotten as have-beens.

The drama of life plays to packed audiences simultaneously every minute of the day or night. Everyone has a chance to act his own part at one time or the other. A stage hand at one time may be a leading actor on another stage the next minute. There is no idle audience. Nature is pretty fair-minded in these matters. Or isn't it? who writes the script? Who assigns the roles? Questions such as these lead down the maze of mysteries. But who can mistake the hands of nature in these things? Evidence? Success, defined as: the hand that works, builds the stage; the brain that thinks, writes the script. But nature abhors equality. The principle of its reward and endowment is based on this: were everyone to be the same height, the same colour and have an equal share of rewards, the rhythm of life would be thrown out of joint; the melody would jar. And life, this life, would stretch from here to nothingness-- devoid of purpose, bereft of meaning.

It, therefore, makes sense that in the drama of life there should be leading actors and actresses who do more than play their own part and depart. Drama, every drama, must have a soul: that soul being those anointed to direct, to lead. Everyone else is a supporting cast, reduced along with the audience, to so many pairs of hands that must clap and applaud the stars who shine and twinkle, turning life's darkness into light; its despair into hope; its hate into love. Even when they depart the stage, they remain, leaping out of the dog-eared pages of history, big brothers and sisters peering at the world from outside the world, daring the world to forget. They leave their footprints on cement cast rather than the sands of time. Neither rain nor the passage of time can obliterate their footprints. Sometimes, lesser men and women try to do so but they only succeed in putting the shine on the march of age.

Unscroll the parchment of history. Julius Caesar, Alexander the Great, Chaka the Zulu, Queen Amina, Adolf Hitler, Winston Churchill, Jesus Christ, Lenin, Mao Tse-Tung, Mohammed. Each of them was and is. The leading actors of life leave only to remain, compelling today to look back to yesterday and learn from those who had acted on various stages before. They are, in effect, the puppeteers who continue to pull the strings of today's social, political and religious behaviour. They are the models for the actors and actresses of today. Their words are the words today's actors and actresses aspire to learn, to assimilate. Their courage is the courage today's actors and actresses want to emulate. It is only in the human world that today is tied to the apron strings of yesterday. See, once again, the hands of nature.

Luck plays a part in life's drama. So does the lack of luck. Time and circumstances call some to the stage at the "right" time among the "right" cast. Being born at the "right" time, in the "right" place and even in the "right" shade of colour can, and does, determine what stage to play on and where. The conspiracy of time and circumstance confers on some actors and actresses undue advantages that make them giants among Lilliputians; men among papier-mache figures.

Flip the coin. The orphans deserted by luck. Being born at the "wrong" time in the "wrong" place among the "wrong" people can be, and often is, an albatross in the drama of life. Some are called out to play their part when the stage is full of bright stars. Their brilliance is lost. They may twinkle but they won't shine. Others are called out to play their part at the "wrong" time. Their efforts are wasted. In life, some strive but they never achieve. It is their luck to sweat and struggle; it is their ill-luck not to be noticed or to be acknowledged only in a footnote on the pages of history. Nature tolerates nothing that disturbs its rhythm, its melody. Even its unfairness.

Nature, really, never gets done with laughing at us. As part of its scheme, it confers on the present the right to pass judgment on the past. Some men and women have that rare combination of luck and ill-luck that they have to listen to the judgment of history on them. They listen, with barely concealed agony, as their past actions and decisions are put through the shredder and a verdict of guilty is handed down to them. Such men and women must wonder, in utter helplessness, why. Some other men and women never wait to hear the judgment of history. Indeed, time and circumstance again do conspire to influence what sort of judgment such men and women will receive. The circumstance and manner of their departure, the timing of their departure -- all these -- either dull the edge of history's sharp knife or replace the knife with a razor blade. Unfair as the judgment of contemporary history may be, there is, like God's judgment, no escaping it.

There is always a consolation. Says David Hart: "There is no gratitude in politics. Past achievements will not solve today's problems." The Right Honourable Dr. Nnamdi Azikiwe, the longest-playing actor in Nigeria's political stage, may wish to drink to that.

Written By Dan Agbese
on November 23, 1987

REPRINTED WITH PERMISSION

PART ONE

* * *

ANCIENT AFRICAN POLITICS AND BELIEFS

Ancient Africans believed in the respect of the elders and "Oneness" of people. Chieftaincy and Kingship were mostly the system of government. Despotism had not been the African way of Kingship or Chieftaincy. Rulers usually consulted the Council of Elders which was a representative body of the villages. They deliberated on issues before they were executed. The deliberation was done extensively as an antidote for eventual and/or inevitable friction and schism.

Some families were made chiefs due to their outstanding respect and behaviour in the society. Their children or close relatives were bestowed on the throne after their fathers, depending on their over-all attitudinal behaviour and wisdom. The functions of the chiefs, among other things, were to act as custodians and judges in both good and bad times; make important decisions that affect, not only the village or town within their immediate domain, but the world beyond. The impartiality of a chief, Oba, or Emir determined his wisdom. In fact, there was no need for the modern day courts then.

Of course, they had checks and balances in their adjudication process. People tried to settle matters within their family units. Where this proved abortive, they could go to their kindred or clan's chief. If this did not work, they could appeal to their village's chief. If the case was still not settled to the satisfaction of the litigants, the council of Elders or chiefs -- Nde Nze-- within the town could make decision on the matter. This gerontocracy was like the present day Supreme Court system. In more cases than note, appellants settled before it reached the final stage.

The ways chiefs, Obas, or Emirs were selected are still very prevalent in African continent today. They still discharge their duties within their immediate domain. The ways Oba of Benin in Bendel State, Obi of Onitsha, Obi of Uburu, Igwe of Amiri, Emirs in the Hausa Land, Oba in Yoruba (all in Nigeria), Zulu in Southern Africa, Kabaka in Uganda, etc. are installed is a pertinent example. It still attracts national attention. In some villages, the presence of police or the court house is not necessary even today, since the villagers can settle their differences amicably with their selected or designated chief presiding. In some cases, modern courts refer litigants to their local chiefs, especially if it pertains to cultural issues or land disputes.

Above all, settlement by the traditional means up to the level of gerontocrats is less costly and more face saving than the present formal legal system.

This was one of the reasons, a few years ago, many young people did not consider law studies when applying for university entrance. Amiri in Oru Local Government Area, Imo State, Nigeria was no exception to this.

When a Police substation was located there (Amiri) about 1976, many people objected to it. They claimed that the presence of the police would make some radical elements in the society to foment trouble. It was also feared that married women would run to the police station when there was little discord within the family. They erroneously speculated that the police station would have a negative impact in the community.

To study law was one of this author's priorities when he graduated from secondary school in 1975. Even his school principal firmly advised him to pursue that relatively prestigious field after witnessing his performance as a defence attorney in the play of "Incorruptible Judge." But his plan was radically changed after he viewed his societal mode. The last straw was when one of his friends and classmates caricatured him that he could be a hungry lawyer in such a sub-culture that did not care much for a formal judicial system. As he pondered over this, he recognized that a significant number of lawyers in Amiri and the neighbouring towns were indeed "hungry lawyers."

But things have changed since then. Youngsters are now encouraged to study beyond law. The once dominant extended-family system is gradually giving way to secularism. Besides, people are now moving to the big cities where the practice of law is much more rewarding. In addition, villages are getting more sophisticated, hence, other amenities and formalities that go with such sophistication. Most villages have now been transformed into towns, and towns into cities, and small cities into large metropolitans. The wave of change never stops. It will continue for better or worse.

POLYGAMY AND SELF-SUFFICIENCY: Ancient Africans believed in self-sufficiency. That, in a way, forced most of them to the aura of polygamy. The larger the family, the more respect the family had, especially if the family had male children. In order for a king, Oba, Zulu, Emir, Kabaka, chief (all symbolizing the same thing) to have dominance over his subjects, he had to have many wives instead of concubines.

By doing this, he was not only gaining respect, but increasing both his political and economic advantage. This does not have anything to do with concupiscence of a man or continence of a woman as new school of thought may imagine.

King Solomon, well known for his wisdom, as noted in the Bible (1st King, chapter 11: 3) had 700 wives and 300 concubines. He would certainly drink to that philosophy.

POLYGAMY AND RELIGION AND CULTURE: In the Africa of old and today, many people who have more than one wife did not do so by the pleasure of polygamous life, but out of necessity. Because of an African standing culture that a man should take the place of his father after his death, many people don't want to have an all-female household. In search of a male, some don't exercise patience with their first wife. Some who do, end up having many children, in the hope that somewhere along the line, there would be a male who could take the mantle from the would-be-retiring father, in perpetuating their family tree and tradition. The so-called X and Y chromosomes syndrome are not in their active vocabulary. As their countries don't have adequate plans for their retirement (old) age, their (male) children provide such social security and insurance.

The advent of churches has not turned this idiosyncratic attitude around either. The churches in most instances had to accommodate this culture. As a Nigerian friend, Patrick E. Williams, simply put it, "Church is a Club." As such, the by-laws of some churches, in some instances have to be moderated to attract members. Besides, there are more churches today than people are willing to attend. In fact, church is more of a business than the altar and sacred place of God.

In addition to studying theology, some clergymen study business as well. Some people go as far as establishing their own church to promote their own ideology, egocentrism, personal satisfaction and philosophical innuendo. This gives strong credibility to the charge that church is now more of a club than religion. In other words, there is now a church for almost every faith, not only in Africa, but world over. Think of Jesu(s) of Oyingbo near Lagos, Olumba Olumba Obu of the Brotherhood of the Cross and Star in Cross River State, Nigeria, Cherubim and Seraphim, Church of Christ of Latter Day Saints, to mention but a few.

Some people are now committing atrocities and abominations under the cloak of religiosity. It is probably appropriate to go beyond Africa at this point. For example, Earl Russel

Behringer, a "pastor" of a church found guilty of capital murder on July 14, 1988 in Fort Worth, Texas, U.S.A., in the 1986 shooting deaths of a couple (who parked on a Mansfield Lovers' Lane), allegedly went to conduct mass an hour after the horrendous act. His accomplice during the murder, who turned state witness, made it possible for his conviction. He tried to use his church's position to camouflage his atrocity of murdering 20-year-old Janet Louise Hancock and her fiance, Daniel Brennan Meyer, Jr., both who were University of Texas at Arlington students, in cold blood. Even if it were his accomplice that pulled the trigger as he claimed during the trial, he had the moral obligation as a clergyman, to report the incident, or at best to prevent it from happening.

What of the alleged murder and death faking by Rev. John Terry in Tennessee State, U.S.A.? According to Newsweek (USA) of September 26, 1988, "The plot was as elaborate and gruesome as a classic film noir." Continued the magazine, "According to police, the Pastor of a Pentecostal congregation in East Nashville Tenn(essee), murdered the church handyman, cut off his head and part of an arm, then set the church on fire with the dismembered body inside. Authorities say that the Rev. John Terry, 44, was hoping the handyman's body would be mistaken for his own; he wanted to start a new life with a new identity, free of his wife -- and enriched by $50,000 in church funds. Everything went as planned, police say, except for one thing: the fire failed to consume the handyman's body. Instead of a pile of charred bones, firemen found a corpse-- one too small to be the large-framed minister. This week the pastor goes on trial for murder.

"Prosecutors, who are seeking the death penalty," said the article, "say Terry planned the crime carefully. Using a name from a tombstone, the pastor allegedly obtained a birth certificate, driver's license and social security card to establish his new identity. Late one night in June 1987, police say, Terry killed James Matheney in the church sanctuary. Prosecutors believe that Terry, a part-time supermarket butcher, severed the head and right arm-- possibly because of an identifying tattoo. He dressed the victim in his own clothes, putting his old I.D. in a pocket. Police figure the pastor made his escape taking the body parts and murder weapon with him."

Unquestionably, this got the church divided. Continued the paper, "Terry surfaced two days after the fire, when police announced they were looking for him. His arrest split the 80-member Emmanuel Church of Christ Oneness Pentecostal." Said Metro Nashville Police Capt. Pat Griffin, "Some of them are sticking with him. They think he's the greatest thing on earth."

Even if he is acquitted by any slim chance by the jury, at least there was a strong probable cause for his murder trial.

What about the prostitution ring operation by some evangelists? Said Dallas Times Herald report of Wednesday, October 12, 1988, "Three evangelists who travel(l)ed the Southern revival circuit pleaded guilty Tuesday (October 11, 1988 in Roanoke, Virginia State, U.S.A.) to running an interstate sex ring of boys they recruited with gifts and money and then molested.

"Tony Leyva, Rias Edward Morris and Freddie Herring" continued the paper, "admitted using Leyva's ministry to recruit boys for homosexual prostitution. Dozens of boys told investigators they were given money, lodging and gifts in return for letting the preachers molest them."

The advent of television gave birth to televangelism. Preachers became millionaires, such as Rev. Jim Bakker of Praise The Lord (PTL), Rev. Jimmy Swaggart who is based in New Orleans, Louisiana, Rev. Jerry Falwell who later formed a political machine called "Moral Majority," Rev. Pat Robertson and his "700 Club" ministry which he aired through his Christian Broadcasting Network, all in the United States of America. The first two, however, were defrocked from their respective denominations for acts of moral turpitude (Bakker for having sex with his secretary (Jessica Hahn) then paid large sums of money in a cover-up skim, and Swaggart for paying a prostitute to pose nude.) Both were married reverends and have fallen from grace to grass.

Even the moslem world has schism in its system of worshipping. In the Northern Nigeria, the centre of African Islamism, army troops had to be dispatched to quell the "warring" factions of Moslems in late 1970s, 1985, 1986 and May 1987. Some lives were lost in the religion-inspired riot against other factions. Their deep contempt against Christians is much worse. Ahmadu Bello University (ABU), Zaria, in the North was closed down on June 13, 1988 to forestall further rioting against the Ibos when an Ibo christian won the presidency of the Students Union. By then one student, Benson Omenka, was dead already. What a shame!! Is this an evidence of "illiteracy" in a university or a mere fanaticism.

In the Persian Gulf, there are radicals and moderates among Moslems. Even in Iran of Ayatollah Ruhollah Khomeini, there was division. Khomeini who overthrew Mohammed Riza Pahlavi, the then Shah of Iran in 1979 in a bloodless religious revolution, and his followers, were extremists who tried to exterminate other tolerable and understanding Moslems. They try to follow the probably God inspired but man-written Koran and man-interpreted Islamic Law to the letter, although selectively. In early 1989, a price tag of over $5 million was placed over the head of Salman Rushdie of Britain (for his death) for writing a book, The Satanic Verses, making mockery of Islam. The death sentence passed on Rushdie who was once a Moslem, was by Ayatollah Khomeini. The world was shocked, especially non-Moslem world.

Egypt, an African country but closer to Middle-East was afraid that such Iranian pugnacious radicalism could spread to her territory. Unfortunately for her, it did, but somewhat minimal. How was President Anwar Sadat assassinated on October 6, 1981, and who was responsible for it? Was it not the act of members of the Moslem fundamentalist organization called Jihad?

Saudi Arabia, due to the fear of the repeat of the riot in Mecca, an Islamic holy city, in 1987, caused mainly by Iranian delegates which claimed over 400 lives, broke up diplomatic relations with Iran on April 26, 1988. That was not surprising, especially after seeing Iranian insistence of toppling Iraq's President Saddam Hussein during their eight year war that started in 1980.

Even in the United States of America, which had "In God We Trust" inscribed on all her currency, including all the denominational coins, there are dichotomous white and black churches. Perhaps there are two colours of God even though there is only one standard colour -- green -- for its legal tender.

The Holy Father (Pope John Paul II) of the Catholic Church in Vatican City, is equally under attack of late on double standard in apportioning blame on violence. The late Rev. (Dr.) Martin Luther King, Jr. in his famous "Letter From Birmingham (Alabama) Jail" written in 1960s, clearly attacked the Catholic Bishops who thought he was asking for too much too soon about civil rights and enfranchisement.

As the Pope went to the Southern sub-region of Africa, which included Zimbabwe and Mozambique, he condemned violence of any kind. He failed to distinguish what kind of violence is tolerable. At least, the violence now staged by the oppressed South African Blacks, particularly the African National Congress which once adopted the late Gandhi of India's system of non-violence, should be distinguished from the pogrom and Nazi style of violence perpetrated by the South African racist government. The defensive, revolutionary and liberating violence of Nelson Mandela, Ho Chi Minh, and perhaps Dr. Sam Nujoma of SWAPO must be separated from the violence of degradation, oppression, repression, exploitation and genocide practiced by Idi Amin Dada, Pieter Botha, Augusto Pinochet of Chile, or Milton Obote of Uganda (his last regime).

When the Pope, real name Karol Wojtyla, formerly Bishop of Krakow, Poland, is not speaking ex-cathedra, which defines papal infallibility, he is believed to sometimes have a double standard as he occupies the position of both the religious and political leadership of the sovereign Vatican-City in Rome. He unequivocally supports the Solidarity Union in his home land Poland which indirectly fights the communist regime of his country, but condemns the activities of the ANC which is desperately fighting for their God given human rights and political enfranchisement. He is alleged of supporting the political participation of priests against the marxist government of his native Poland, while at the same time condemning the participation of priests in the marxist government of Nicaragua (perhaps with good reasons for Nicaragua) and some other places.

According to Dr. Patrick F. Wilmot on September 26, 1988, ". . . Christians in general, and Catholics in particular, there should be no crisis of conscience in supporting the just struggle for daily bread, human dignity, equality, and happiness. After all, this is what christianity is supposed to be all about. Until we inherit the Kingdom of heaven, we have the right to protect ourselves on this one. We must give unto Caesar the things that are Caesar's, even if these flow out of cannons, recoilless rifles and machine guns."

The Vatican has modified its stand on South African issues, particularly on racism and apartheid; and it is in writing too.

In a document titled "The Church and Racism: Towards A More Fraternal Society" released on Friday, February 10, 1989, it described racism as "wound in humanity's side," and apartheid as "the most marked and systematic form" of racism. The document stressed that economic sanctions against South Africa could be justified because of its unrelenting apartheid system.

It was said that Pope John Paul, II had the Vatican's Justice and Peace Commission prepare the document to help "enlighten and awaken consciences".

The Commission said it was not trying to "gloss over the weaknesses and even, at times, the complicity" of the Roman Catholic Church in racism throughout history, and declared that the church "wants first and foremost to change racist attitudes, including those within her own communities."

Much credit should be given to Cardinal Roger Etchegaray of France who headed the Commission that prepared the document. He said that the document reflected his observations during a two-week tour of South Africa in 1988. It is now nice to hear that the Catholic Church has spoken out against racism, apartheid, and gross inequality, inequity, and injustice in the world; a cause the Rev. (Dr.) Martin Luther King, Jr. fought and died for in the United States of America.

SUPREME BEING: Although Ancient Africans believed in the Supreme Being, they equally had some deities or personal gods that acted as intermediary between them and the Almighty God, just like some christians, namely Catholics, pray to God mostly through Jesus Christ, Angel Gabriel, or Virgin Mary. There were other smaller gods like god of thunder, god of sun, god of harvest, god of rain, and what have you. They prayed to the Omni-Scient through these self-made gods.

They believed in reincarnation too. In fact, most still do irrespective of any religious affiliation. The Bible even implies that there is reincarnation. It is widely believed within the christian enclave that John The Baptist was the reincarnation of Prophet Elijah.

What about Jesus Christ? Did he come through the reincarnation of Moses or God Himself, through the "Virgin" Mary, the wife of Joseph, son of Jacob? (Joseph was the son of Jacob -- Matthew 1:16).

Said Olumba Olumba Obu of Nigeria, the founder and leader of Brotherhood of the Cross and Star as reported in the African Guardian of May 16, 1988, ". . . The judgment, the divine rulership has begun. Everything is turning new leaf. By this doctrine the Brotherhood of the Cross and Star therefore holds that when God the Spirit first became flesh, He was known as Adam; the first Alpha. Adam was taken unto God, came back the second time and was called Enoch. Enoch was taken unto God and came back as Noah. Noah was taken unto God and came back in another age as Melchizedek. Melchizedek was taken unto God and came back the next age as Moses. Moses was taken unto God and came back the next generation as Elijah, who reincarnated as John The Baptist. Then Christ was taken to God, promised us the comforter (himself) will come back again. The promised comforter or christ arrived on earth as Olumba Olumba Obu (O.O.O.) . . ."

To sort out the intricacies surrounding religious mysteries, perhaps needs to be left for the students and scholars of theology.

Due to the respect Africans had for

one another, particularly people of the same tribe or clan, things were in harmony. Judicial cases were expeditiously adjudicated amicably in most instances. They established other cultural traditions that stabilized their day-to-day activities. They used certain tap-roots, selected tree stems and leaves for medication; they still do. The native doctors cured various diseases and sicknesses. In fact, their native medicine gave birth to the modernized medicine which the West or the so-called developed world hardly give them the overdue credit and recognition.

Native doctors in Africa can force rain to fall or stop rain from falling. One native doctor from Umuduru Amiri named Ugo (Eagle in literary English meaning) Nwaizu is one of many native doctors that can do that. During a rare interview with this author, Ugo whom age is now taking a toll, on a cool Wednesday evening of February 24, 1988, confided with a certain degree of honesty and confidence to the interviewer that he has an innate ability to force down or restrain rain. According to him, the innate power originated from his maternal great-great-grandfather. His mother came from a neighbouring town called Omuma, very much known within the environs, perhaps erroneously, for their voodoo practice and suspicion of one another.

When asked if he would be willing to

teach the younger generation how to practice this unique voodoo, or can it be called art, since he was naturally aging, his answer was unequivocally yes. However, he cautioned that there are some terrible inherent risks involved. He told this in Igbo proverb. Literarily interpreted, he said that "UBUBURU" -- a stinging insect -- "uses a mat to carry its new born to its bosom, but an ordinary creature which could be stung, by mere ignorance is trying to carry the new born with bare hands."

This metaphoric saying, when interpreted, simply means that he himself who uses supernatural power to force down or restrain rain has been trying to no avail to get out of it, a young person who does not know the intricacies of the aftermath dares to join the affray.

This Ugo man is tough. You dare not take any of his personal effects, or enter into his property without permission. If you dare do otherwise, you can literally be either stung by bees, suffer some rashes on your body, or be walking around the property hallucinating until he meets you in person.

As a matter of fact, his immediate family is in disarray. His two sons successively became lunatics at relatively young ages and wandered away. His female child never settled to a form of valid marriage. As all his sons were wasted due to an unknown phenomenon, he has no one to carry his enviable mantle after him, except his daughter. The irony of it is that he can make an impotent woman to bear baby by administering native medicine. His daughter though has children. Now one can understand why he would like to but not enthusiastically train someone else to do what he does best -- force down or restrain rain, among other activities.

One might rightly ask, if Africans can force down rain, why is there drought and barren land in some African countries like Ethiopia? Native Dr. Ugo Nwaizu told the author during the informal interview that he uses certain leaves to perform the function. In addition, he uses a certain "Okute" -- stone -- which is readily available. His *ofo*, intuitively should not be excluded. During the dry season (which was the season at the time of this interview) the leaves wither away. He has to wait until they grow back. However, he can use other alternative means to force down the rain, but the consequences would be catastrophic. The cost could range from property to human destruction through uncontrollable thunderous activities.

He muttered that a prophet is usually not recognized in his home town. He was ostensibly, though indirectly, referring to an incident that happened in

Umuduru village in mid-1970s. It was reported that in June 1975 when the community had its annual Oghu (pronounced as Owu) Festival, it did not want rain to disrupt the grand occasion. June is usually a rainy month in Nigeria. As such, the executives of the Oghu Festival went to a neighbouring town -- Omuma-- to forestall the rain till after this important occasion by paying homage to a well-known native doctor.

This backfired because they neglected Dr. Ugo, a native son in their midst. Due to the possession of his unseen power, Ugo is perceived to be a little insane at times. He soliloquizes most often. He is a lonely man. But he is always cognizant of all the traditional rituals and festivities, including religious ceremonies. He was terribly upset and furious when he heard what the executives did. He promised a rainy day.

A few hours before the occasion would kick off, Ugo set off rain. It rained all day. The people could not fathom what went awry until it occurred to one elderly man that the rain was the handiwork of Ugo. A few people were sent to appease him. He did not hide his disappointment and embarrassment of by-passing him to go to a neighbouring town. He reluctantly dismantled his "mechanical" work. The rain stopped. The festivity belatedly started with unpleasant ranco(u)r and blame.

During another occasion in the town, the neglect was repeated. Apparently they did not learn a sufficient lesson from the previous incident. This time he allowed people to reach the scene of the festivity, only to set off rain. The rain was only at the scene of the festivity while sunshine glittered around the town. People started running helter-skelter. It must be noted here that the Oghu dance is performed in an organized open field. Once again, the Doctor had to be appeased, this time with substantial fee. Since then he was accorded his respect as a true native doctor.

Please note that this is not a fairy tale. It is a true story. At the time of this writing, he is still alive and has not passed his knowledge to someone else. As implied in his proverbial pronouncement, some people would not want to get involved, either due to certain religious mentality or the enormous and inherent excruciating risks embodied with the act. The provenance of his demeaning power came from his maternal heritage. Perhaps partly paternal.

Ironically though, it is the fear of change, modernization or assumption of risk that has continually kept the African continent dragging. Some of the African cultures, unfortunately, were destroyed or taken away by their colonial masters. And the modern rulers, after getting the independence, blindly followed the footsteps of the Europeans without blending the African rich cultures with the developed world's technology. Thus, injustice to African cultures set in. No strong concern was legitimately given to the African style of doing things. A power struggle took off. Everyone wanted to grab power at all costs. Opposition and dissent were and still are crushed. Every rule of political and moral decency is now flouted. Materialism quickly overshadowed the idea of "oneness." Nobody is the brother's keeper anymore.

Individualism or the so-called secular system has overcome the collectivism which makes people to be more concerned with group or community activities than personal remuneration. Thus, envy, partiality, corruption, indiscipline, tribalism, incompetence, economic and research stagnation, and above all, the present and ever evolving political unrest in Africa -- a continent historians and scientists generally agree was the provenience and first call of homo sapiens -- set afoot.

Whether all these will be overcome, much less eradicated, is left for the present and future generations to decide and act upon. Of course, their concern will determine the outcome. Again, the fate is on "Mr. Hope."

* * *

SLAVERY AND COLONIZATION AT A GLANCE

The worst situation that befell Africa was the colonization by the Europeans. Before colonization, however, the Africans had advanced culturally. Things were running smoothly, especially in the powerful areas of the continent, irrespective of the sporadic inter-tribal wars.

The Africans were enticed into the disdainful colonization by the establishment of trade links and/or religious relationships with the Arabs at first, and later Europeans. The Arabs eventually came with Islamism while the Europeans brought with them christianity in the form of missionary works.

The missionaries from Europe acted like charitable samaritans. They were followed by established businessmen who came with their government backing. Europeans started offering aid and protection. The trade link seemed genuine until they commenced trading and kidnapping of human beings among other things.

African nations were in the form of

Empires with fortified armies during the early centuries. Sometimes they fought among themselves in search of power and dominance. The most powerful, although at various times, in West Africa, according to historians, were Mali, Ghana, Benin, Songhai, and Ashanti empires, among others. In the Southern and Central Africa were Luba Kingdoms, Lund Empire, the Rozwi Empire of Zimbabwe, to name a few.

In the land between Songhai and Kanem-Bornu, lay Hausa communities of Gobir, Daura, Katsina, Zaria, Kano, Rano, and Biram. The Hausa States never became a Hausa empire. They, however, developed into strong commercial centres due to the Arab trade. In about 1400 A.D., the Hausa kings embraced Islam. Since then, the area became an important centre of Islamic culture and religion that we see there today.

Another empire worth mentioning was the Oyo Empire. However, it disintegrated in the 19th century because of civil war brought about mainly due to the European slave trade.

Ashanti Empire arose toward the end of the 17th century in the Akan forest lands between the coast and the Volta River.

Under Osei Tutu, Ashanti people were spiritually united by a sacred symbol, the Golden stool. As their sacred lore had it, "It had come from Nyame, the Supreme God, and had been obtained through the magic powers of Anotchi Okomfo Anokye, the greatest doctor in the land. He had caused it to descend through thick black clouds roaring with thunder, and when the Golden stool came to rest on Osei Tutu's knees, he became the Asantehene, the head of the Ashanti nation . . ." When Osei Tutu died in the battlefield in 1717, his nephew, Opuku Ware, took over the vast empire and continued his policy of expansion to Cape Mount, in the present-day Liberia, Dahomey (now Benin Republic),, etc. Like other African empires, it became involved in the 18th century war which required the acquisition of European firearms. It also got involved in the slave trade. Ashanti was eventually overthrown by the British in 1825. The Ashanti tribe is now part of the present Ghana nation.

Most African Empires arose at different times. Some arose by the downfall of another. The Europeans were well aware of the strengths and powers of the Africans in both wars and physique. They could not attempt to carry war to them in fear of summary defeat. Thus, they used diplomacy.

As such, they started with missionary work that led to the emergence of christianity in Africa. The Asians introduced Moslem faith, particularly at the Northern side, while the Europeans, in apparent competition, invaded the southern part with christianity. The irony is that both religions were used as shields for the real intent of the Europeans and Arabs, particularly Great Britain. The coming of the missionaries and later businessmen, were chartered, and in some cases financed by the British government. Ever since decolonization though, Great Britain is no more "great"; rather it follows in the shadow of the United States of America which it once colonized.

As it has been noted earlier, the missionaries started giving misguided aids and protection to the strong empires. Without realizing that it was a trick, the Africans who were ambivalent of the whitemen, started giving them open arms. With the open arms, came their penetration into the society. They quickly learned African strengths and weaknesses. The Africans did not realize that there was no and still there is no free lunch. The offering of aid and protection was just an enticement as well as seducement and entrapment. The aborigines had to pay for them later through degradation and slavery.

The first set of Africans that went to some European countries and the New World were indentured servants. When they were told about the opportunities in America -- the New World -- they tried to explore the uncharted waters, with the intention of eventually going back to their respective mother land. Through their adventure, they found out that it was easier to go to the New World than come back. They ended up settling at their respective destinations at the whims and caprices of their then friends.

As the cooperation in business with the indigenes was progressing, the Europeans were eyeing beyond friendship. By helping the powerful empires to dethrone the fledgling ones, the Europeans gained by taking the prisoners of war as a reward for their, sometimes unsolicited, aids. They took the most able people of the dethroned empires. This was never easy though. In some instances, they had to fight with the host over the prisoners of war. In Africa then, prisoners of war were enslaved by the victors.

The Kingdom of Benin in Nigeria was known for its steadfastness against the Europeans. Oba Ovonranwen Nogbaisi of Benin resisted strongly when the British really meant to overrun his kingdom. He was later bundled into exile in Calabar (now part of Cross River State in Nigeria) where he died a completely wasted and frustrated man in 1929. King Jaja of Opobo, an Ibo (or Igbo) man, equally fought valiantly for his relatively small kingdom. But you could hardly go beyond a certain level of valour with mere bows and arrows, spears and machetes over guns and bullets. The use of *egbe ntu*, otherwise known as "dane gun," was later invented by Africans to compete against the European superior technology. By this time, it was too late. They had been outgunned and subdued. They succumbed, but reluctantly. Some of the creative arts and sculptures kept in the kingdoms were forcefully taken.

In 1977 when Nigeria hosted the Second World Black Festival of Arts and Culture, dubbed FESTAC '77, the Nigerian Government officially requested the "stolen" Benin sculptures from their once colonial master, Britain, but to no avail. Nigeria eventually had to settle for replicas over the original art work.

It must be mentioned here though, that there were relatively few known kingdoms in the Igbo land (of Nigeria), among which (existed) were Opobo and Aruchukwu. Aruchukwu was the most powerful and the last known Igbo Kingdom in Nigeria, although it never became an empire. It was where the Igbos or Ibos of all clans used to go to talk to Chukwu (The God Almighty) when they had highly irreconcilable disputes of importance. Some who went to "talk to Chukwu" never came back. The mysterious explanation to that was "Chukwu took (killed) them."

Aruchukwu itself, like other

powerful kingdoms and empires, engaged in slave trade. It failed to acknowledge the fact that slave trade had legally ended around the world in the 1800's. They used to kidnap some of those who came to "talk to Chukwu" and sell them into slavery, although officially they explained that Chukwu had taken the person(s). Aruchukwu was only defeated in the 19th century and the Kingdom disbanded by the West African Frontier Force set up by its former principal customer, Britain.

In fact, the Ibos in general, according to history, were the most democratic in West Africa. They did not, and still do not believe that only one family or one person would forever rule. They liked, and still like to elect the best qualified person at a particular time to ensure dynamism and continuous development which, in most cases, come as a result of new ideas and new trials. And they were always open to new changes, ideas, and adventures irrespective of their war victories. That is why it is said "*Igbo ekwe eze,*" an Igbo idiomatic expression, meaning Ibos do not believe in "perpetual" kings or rulers, otherwise known as president-for-life.

This probably is why, unlike the Yorubas and Hausas in Nigeria, they do not pay obeisance to a living person. This relatively late culture, in most cases, is misunderstood by other tribes as a sign of disobedience or arrogance.

Perhaps, because of all these and their enterprising abilities, the Ibos were, and still are seen at any major and/or reputable cities in Nigeria, and to some extent, other countries of the world, engaged in commercial ventures or professional careers. Wherever they are, they always have strong ties to their roots.

Their receptiveness or openness to changes was equally why, when christianity with its education and westernization came to Africa, it permeated very quickly into that part (East) of Nigeria. Perhaps that, among other things, was the reason some of their African compatriots call them the Jews of Africa.

However, those Africans taken as slaves were not only those defeated in the tribal wars. In some localities, people with dissenting ideas or radical opinions, or persons viewed as strong opponents to the ruling class in Africa, would be sold or given away to the merchants. As a matter of fact, some of those sold were the most healthy. Even people who disobeyed their parents or did not act the way their parents wanted them to act, would be given away. Being sold as a slave was looked upon as vengeance or calculated punishment by either the parents or the community. In addition to men of goodwill, bad ones were also sold. Those who were perceived as hanky-panky, or double agents in attitudinal manifestation or conduct, were equally given away.

Within Africa, as the prevailing culture before the arrival of the Europeans, there was some kind of existing slavery. Mungo Park who travelled in west Africa (he discovered River Niger at last in Nigeria after Richard Lander's attempt) between 1795 and 1797 observed that people could become slaves, not only through captivity but equally through famine, insolvency, and crimes.

In the time of famine, some families gave their daughters in marriage or their sons as labourers, in exchange of corn, millet, or other food items to save their family members from starvation. In the eyes of foreigners, these daughters and sons had been sold into slavery. Africans though, did not consider them as slaves in their eyes. In those days, if a man incurred debts and became insolvent, not only would his personal property be sold to satisfy the creditors, but also his very person. According to Mungo Park, this was the most common cause of "slavery" in Africa. People who committed crimes, such as murder, adultery, and witchcraft could either be stoned to death or sold away for good.

The aborigines did not know what was behind the mind of the Europeans when they were engaged into the real slave trade. As people with dissenting opinions and/or perceived as a threat to the aristocracy or oligarchy (whichever that applied) were either sold, given away or at worst killed, the society was left with more and more of less powerfuls. As experience would show, those who hardly question anything are looked upon as obedient. But they are not necessarily smarter. Naturally, human beings don't like opposition. They usually think that by eliminating the opposition the problems would be solved. This is hardly so. The reason, in part, is that tomorrow's problems may not be solved by today's ideas. And the society must in one way or another pay for such asininity.

Nonetheless, as the Europeans see that the remaining people were not all that powerful anymore and the population had substantially decreased, they overran the countries and reduced the natives to servitude. That was the beginning of colonization -- the 19th century scramble for Africa -- which was formalized through the European "Berlin Conference" of 1884-85.

The conference was to have the common understanding of their scramble, so that they would not start to fight against themselves in a foreign land. As it can be seen, Europeans were no longer contented with taking Africans into far off lands, but laid claim to their very soil and forcefully took possession of the land itself.

To perpetuate their avariciousness, they denied the so-called western education to the people, to avoid any strong opposition to their inevitable exploitation. The only kind of education later made available, of course, out of necessity, was the English language, French or Spanish, depending on which European country was the colonial master. The main purpose for this was to have natives as interpreters or translators to the local chiefs.

In most areas, they instituted the divide-and-rule indignant system. The History of the Europeans and not Africans, geography, literature, and a few other social science courses were later taught. Before this, original African schools had been demolished. Africans were from then on taught what the Europeans wanted them to know and not what they wanted to learn.

Courses, such as law, business, engineering, economics, management, to mention just a few, were not taught in fear of enlightening the people.

The manufacture of goods was done in

the home base of the colonial masters. The colonial masters exploited not only the people they took as slaves, and the citizens they had reduced to second class, but the God given natural resources and cash crops in Africa.

They would take the cash crops or raw materials to their home base, manufacture them to the finished products and then resold them to these same countries at exorbitant prices. Remember that the raw materials were purchased at give-away prices set by the colonial masters. If the imperialists were so caring, why did they not establish manufacturing companies in these countries. They obviously foresaw that they must go someday. The trick worked. It resulted in a snob-appeal attitude that necessitated African nations to be a dumping ground to date, instead of being at least among the new industrialized countries (NIC).

There is no doubt that some African cultures died out due to the colonization. Their original philosophy of being the brother's keeper, collectivism, and enterprising were superseded with haphazard "protection" and token aid. Ever since then, Africa has not been the Africa of the old. They are now centuries behind in this fast changing world. The clock is ticking, faster, at their chagrin. Unknown countries centuries ago, now lead and control the world. The African continent, the origin of mankind, is now begging for help. Help of what and from who?

If Africa is allowed to write an epitaph of itself on its present predicament for the developed world to see, it might read thus: As you are now, so I wanted to be; as I am now, so I want you to taste.

* * *

POLITICAL INDEPENDENCE

To gain back political independence from the colonial masters was one of the greatest challenges Africans had ever faced. To push the Europeans away from the continent they were exploiting for their economic boom and boon seemed impossible. Many Africans who had the opportunity to acquire western education started noticing the true colours of the Europeans. They began to find out that the Europeans never intended to be a Messiah, but more or less exploiters and opportunists, eager to satisfy their own amphibiousness. The erudition of these young Africans made them to demand self-government for the eventual benefit of their countries and the continent. Some old chiefs who were influenced by the European gifts were against the independence at first, until they were enlightened at last.

Dr. Nnamdi Benjamin Azikiwe who studied in the United States of America between 1925 and 1934, during the height of segregation and non-person treatment of the Black Race in that country, came back to Nigeria to fight for independence. His best ammunition, in addition to his impeccable credentials was his pen. With various degrees and diplomas from various institutions of higher learning in the segregated colleges and universities in the United States of America, among which were the University of Pennsylvania where he received a Master's in Anthropology and International Law, Lincoln University where he received a Bachelor of Science in Political Science and a Master's in Philosophy and Religion (he taught at Lincoln too), Columbia University (diploma in Journalism), and Howard University, he was well equipped for the task ahead.

He continued from where others, like Herbert Marculey who died in 1944 left. The irony was that his home country, ran by the British, was very fragile for his intended revolution. Like independent Liberia and Ethiopia which simultaneously turned down his application to work in their foreign ministry, his country, which was run by the British expatriates, couldn't even offer him a journalistic position. He then left for Accra, Gold Coast (now Ghana) where he became the Editor-In-Chief of the African Morning Post until 1937 when he was charged and convicted of sedition, along with Isaac Wallace-Johnson, due to their fearless attack of the white despotic rulers. He did not have any better alternative than to have a triumphant return to his home country after serving his brief time in jail. On his return to Nigeria, he mobilized the youths behind him and formed the West African Pilot, among other newspapers, as the vocal mouthpiece of the people.

This was not an easy affair though. You can imagine that from what is happening at the present time in the "Republic" of South Africa, where 25 million blacks cannot vote in the national election that determines their future. Four million whites at the time of this writing rule and dictate their fate. The blacks were and still are disfranchised. It is left to be seen where the wave of change will take them in South Africa.

Nigeria, however, got her independence on October 1, 1960. The Honorable Dr. Nnamdi Azikiwe was lucky to be alive to be named her first and only indigenous Governor-General, and subsequently, the President and Commander-in-Chief of the Armed Forces when Nigeria became a Republic in 1963 under a parliamentary system.

In his speech when he was sworn in, he unequivocally said, among other things, "Let us serve this nation loyally and faithfully, with determination to preserve and protect the rights and obligation enshrined in the constitution of our new Republic. In doing so, we shall give faith to the skeptic, infuse courage in the timid and restore hope to the disillusioned."

On the Nigerian independence, Azikiwe, of course, was not the only nationalist, although his prolificity and forensic characteristics, coupled with his unrivalled credentials put him atop any one before him. Many of the pioneers, such as Herbert Marculey, fought relentlessly for the independence. It was unfortunate that he did not see it through. There were some unknowns who died in the pursuit of this inevitable freedom and self-government. An example of such persons was Heelas Ugokwe, a 25-year-old returnee from World War II who joined the Zikist Movement. A Post and Telegraph (P&T) staffer, Ugokwe in 1950, with a jack knife, attacked the Government Chief Secretary, Mr. H. M. Foot in an assassination attempt. He was jailed for 12 years. He was released after six years, but contracted tuberculosis while in jail. He died two years after his release.

Among others who lived to see it fulfilled included the late Chief Obafemi Awolowo, Sir (Dr.) Francis (later Dr. Akanu) Ibiam, late Chief Mbonu Ojike, late Dr. Jaja Wachukwu, late Dr. Michael I. Okpara, late Mallam (later Alhaji) Aminu Kano, Margaret Ekpo, late Alhaji Abubaker Tafawa Balewa, Chief Anthony Enahoro, late Chief Festus Okotie-Eboh,

Dr. Kinsley O. Mbadiwe, to mention but a few.

Those who fought valiantly and relentlessly, directly or indirectly for the Nigerian independence but were lost in the course of history included Michael Aitokhaimen Omiunu Imoudu, born on September 17, 1902, who in 1941 led the Railway workers on strike over "Cost of living Allowance," and in 1945, spearheaded a general strike that lasted 44 days, after he served a two-year jail term for his action of 1941; former Emir of Zaria, Aliyu dan Sidi who was deposed by Lord Lugard and sent into exile to Lokoja, due to an "offence" of writing a poem denouncing colonialism and British adventurism; late Alhaji Raji Abdallah who was jailed for two years for delivering a "seditious" lecture at Glover Hall in Lagos in 1949; the late Fumilayo Ransome-kuti who died in 1978, not by the hand of the British she stood up against, but by the Nigerian Military during the reign of her home-boy -- Gen. Olusegun Obasanjo; and others like Private Theo Ayoola (soldier); Mohammadu Allangade (soldier); Lawan Dambazau, Ikenna Nzimiro (now professor of Sociology), M. C. K. Ajuluchukwu, Nduka Eze, late Saad Zungur, Chief Mokwugo Okoye, Osita Agwuna, Fred Anyiam, Tanko Yakassai, T. O. S. Benson (a jurist), M. T. Mbu, Hajia Sawaba Gambo, to mention but only few. As it can be seen from the prefix, only a few are still alive.

Other countries in Africa suffered the same fate as Nigeria. The late Dr. Kwame Nkrumah of Ghana (formerly Gold Coast) under his charismatic leadership, led Ghana to independence. Although Nigerians started the struggle for independence first from the colonial master Britain, Ghana obtained hers before Nigeria from the same Britain. Ghana gained her independence on March 6, 1957. The British was believed to have prolonged the handover of power to Nigerians, in part because of Northern Nigeria reluctance to cooperate with the highly educated Ibos from the East and Yorubas from the West.

During a conference in London in the early 1950's to determine the process of gradual handover of power, the Sardauna of Sokoto, Sir (Alhaji) Ahmadu Bello, an Hausa leader, to the astonishment of his fellow Nigerians, announced that Nigerians were not ready to govern themselves yet. He figured that the Ibos and Yorubas who were the Nigerian elites then, particularly a figure like Nnamdi Azikiwe and his henchmen from the East, would deprive them a good place in the seat of the Nigerian government. In fact, he proposed a nine-cardinal point plan in which Nigeria could be independent. Among them was confederation which meant splitting Nigeria into three semi-independent nations according to the three major tribes, so that the Hausa, which was the major source of cash crops that yielded foreign reserves then, could govern itself. Nobody knew that petroleum which would supersede other cash crops could be discovered in the Eastern Region a few years later. This proposal was summarily rejected in favour of one Nigeria. The British capitalized on this to prolong the independence.

Another underlying reason for the delay of the overdue freedom was to penalize and punish Nigerians for initiating the struggle for the continent's total emancipation. The Nigerian nationalists were viewed as unnecessarily too pedantic, smart and belligerent for their goal.

It must be recalled that Nkrumah, like Azikiwe, studied in the United States of America. He was believed to be the protege of Dr. Azikiwe, although with different idiosyncratic styles. Zik was very accommodating, flexible or chameleonic; Dr. Nkrumah, like Zik's arch rival in Nigeria, the late Chief Obafemi Awolowo, was not. (Chief Awolowo supposedly died naturally on May 9, 1987.)

However, Nnamdi Azikiwe, famously known as ZIK of Africa, explained in the Daily Times of Nigeria of June 23, 1979 on his flexibility or compromise stance this way: "Compromise is the art of symbiotic living, hence the most successful politicians are those who compromise for the common good whilst not sacrificing fundamental principles."

In September 1987, in response to a news reporter's question about the same issue during his courtesy call to General Ibrahim B. Babangida (Nigerian Military President) he said, "We made some compromise to allow the nation to succeed. Without compromise, could this world progress? When two incompatibles meet, they co-exist by agreeing to agree on certain issues and agreeing to disagree on other issues. This has been my guideline all my life." Certainly, President Ronald Wilson Reagan of the United States of America, who described the Soviet Union as "Evil Empire" as late as 1985, and Mikhail Gorbachev, the General-Secretary and the leader of the U.S.S.R., will strongly agree to that eloquent and chivalrous dictum during their INF (Intermediate Nuclear Force Freeze) summit held in Washington, D.C., capital of the U.S.A. from December 7-10, 1987 and subsequently in Moscow, Soviet Union, from May 29 to June 2, 1988.

The first African independent country was Liberia. It was given its independence on July 26, 1847. This was so because the United States of America, tired of the enslaved Africans' demand for freedom and the subsequent abolition of slavery in 1808, decided to free them. They were sent to that African site and named it Liberia (Liberty). It must be noted, however, that Ethiopia, formerly under the name of ABYSSINIA, was never colonized by any power. It claims to have been independent since 11th century B. C. Since its existence, irrespective of some wars, it had been the master of its fate. Emperor Haile Selassie I, crowned in 1930, whose original name was RAS TAFARI MAKONNEN, incorporated other suburbs near Ethiopia and called all the area Ethiopia. The Ethiopia it answers is the same Ethiopia of the christian biblical knowledge, but the old Ethiopia was under Abyssinia State. Haile Selassi I, claimed to be a descendant of the Queen of Sheba, and to some degree, King Solomon.

Other African nations that have had their independence to date, in order of the attainment, are:

2. Egypt, February 28, 1922
3. Libya, December 24, 1951
4. Sudan, January 1, 1956
5. Morocco, March 2, 1956
6. Tunisia, March 20, 1956
7. Ghana, March 6, 1957
8. Guinea, October 2, 1958
9. Cameroon, January 1, 1960
10. Togo, April 27, 1960
11. Mali, June 20, 1960
12. Senegal, June 20, 1960
13. Madagascar, June 26, 1960

14. Zaire (as the Congo Leopoldville) June 30, 1960
15. Somalia, July 1, 1960
16. Benin (as Dahomey) August 1, 1960
17. Niger, August 3, 1960
18. Burkina Faso (as Upper Volta) August 5, 1960
19. Ivory Coast (Cote d' Ivoire) August 7, 1960
20. Chad, August 11, 1960
21. The Central African Republic (CAR), August 13, 1960
22. Peoples Republic of Congo or The Congo (formerly Congo Brazzaville), August 15, 1960
23. Gabon, August 17, 1960
24. Nigeria, October 1, 1960
25. Mauritania, November 28, 1960
26. Sierra Leone, April 27, 1961
27. Tanzania (as Tanganyika) December 9, 1961
28. Rwanda, July 1, 1962
29. Burundi, July 1, 1962
30. Algeria, July 3, 1962
31. Uganda, October 9, 1962
32. Zanzibar (now part of Tanzania), December 10, 1963
33. Kenya, December 12, 1963
34. Malawi, July 6, 1964
35. Zambia, October 24, 1964
36. The Gambia, February 18, 1965
37. Botswana, September 30, 1966
38. Lesotho, October 4, 1966
39. Mauritius, March 12, 1968
40. Swaziland, September 6, 1968
41. Equatorial Guinea, October 12,

1968
42. Guinea Bissau, September 10, 1974
43. Mozambique, June 25, 1975
44. Cape Verde, July 5, 1975
45. The Comoros, July 6, 1975
46. Sao Tome & Principe, July 12, 1975
47. Angola, November 11, 1975
48. Seychelles, June 29, 1976
49. Djibouti, June 27, 1977
50. Zimbabwe, April 18, 1980
51. *Sahrawi Arab Democratic Republic (also known as Western Sahara), supposedly May 22, 1976
52. Namibia, April 1, 1990 according to treaties signed at the UN on December 22, 1988

* The independence of the Saharawi Arab Democratic Republic, largely known as Western Sahara, which was admitted into the Organization of African Unity (OAU) in February 1982, is still being disputed by Morocco which claims the island in defiance of the International Courts of Justice at the Hague's ruling in October 1975 in favour of independence and self-determination of the people of Western Sahara. The courts vehemently ruled that neither Morocco, nor Mauritania (which also claimed the territory) was entitled to claim sovereignty over the territory and that its people had the right to self-determination. Both had earlier pledged

to abide by the finding of the courts. Now, only Morocco renegaded it.

Because of the admittance, Morocco withdrew from the Organization (OAU) in November 1985. Although the Sahrawi Arab Democratic Republic was admitted by 26 of the 50 members, Morocco disputed the membership, claiming with some other countries, that two-thirds majority is needed to admit a state whose existence was in question. The government of SADR, even though in disarray due to Moroccan warfare against her, is presently recognized by 69 nations. Mohammed Abdel Aziz was the president at this writing.

There are a total of about 51 relatively independent countries in Africa. It could increase to 52 if Namibia is actually liberated from the crunches of racist South Africa as expected on April 1, 1990. (The South African Army started its pull out from Namibia on April 1, 1989. The U.N. flag was mounted there on the same April 1, 1989. Elections are slated for November, 1989. The full independence of Namibia is April 1, 1990.) The number may even shrink if the smaller countries merge with relatively economically stronger neighbours as Zanzibar did with Tanzania, and as Gambia might do if necessitated, with Senegal to be "Senegambia."

The Republic of South Africa is quite all right an independent country.

Outline Political Map of Contemporary Africa

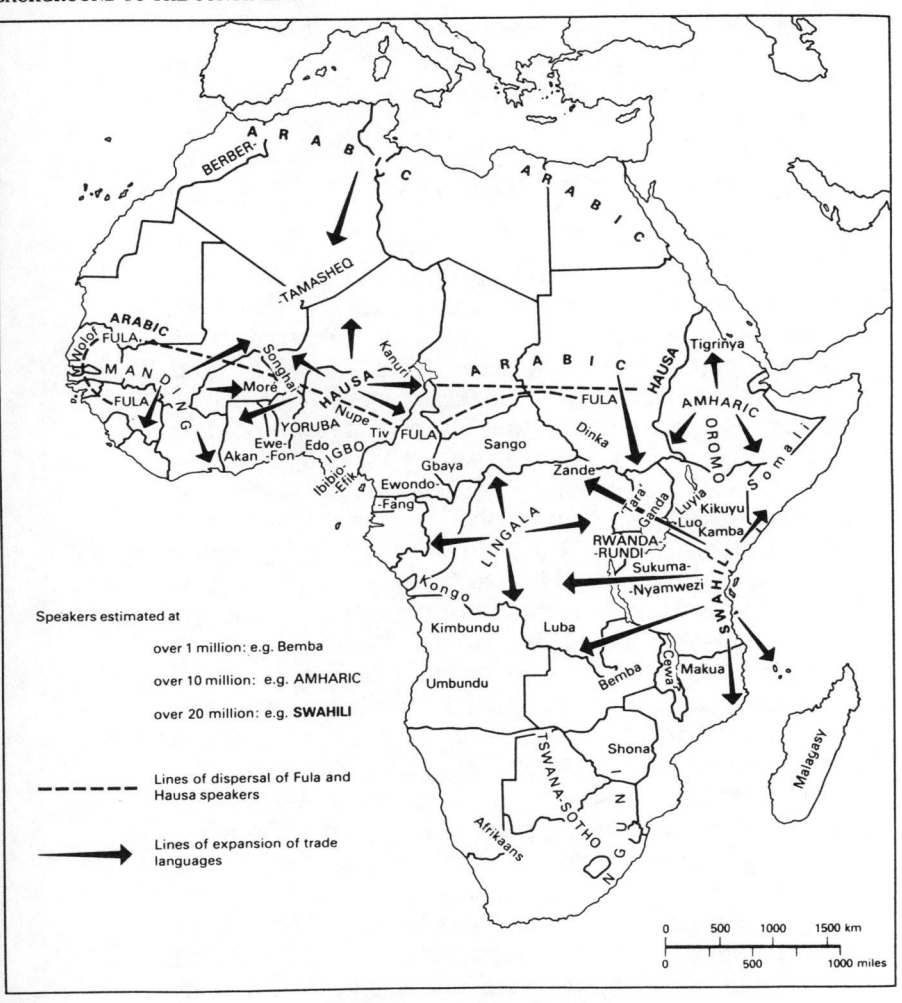

BACKGROUND TO THE CONTINENT　　　　　　　　　　　　　　　　　*African Languages*

Map 1: Major Languages in Africa

Major languages within the Northern Area of Wider Affinity ("Hamito-Semitic"): **ARABIC**, AMHARIC, BERBER-TAMASHEQ, **HAUSA**, OROMO (=GALLA), Somali, Tigrinya.

Major languages within the Southern Area of Wider Affinity ("Niger-Congo"): Akan (=Twi-Fante), Edo, Ewe-Fon, FULA (=FULANI), Gbaya, Ibibio-Efik, IGBO, Moré (=Mossi), Nupe, Sango, Tiv, Wolof, YORUBA, Zande and the following Bantu languages: Bemba, Cewa (=Nyanja), Ewondo-Fang, Ganda, Kamba, Kimbundu, Kongo, LINGALA, Luba, Luyia, Makua, NGUNI (incl. Zulu-Xhosa-Swati-Ndebele), RWANDA-RUNDI, Shona, **SWAHILI**, Sukuma-Nyamwezi, "Tara" (=Kiga-Nkore-Tooro-Nyoro), TSWANA-SOTHO, Umbundu.

Other languages: Afrikaans, Dinka, Kanuri, Luo, Malagasy, MANDING (=Malinké-Bambara-Dyula), Songhai and the following European languages, not shown on map: **ENGLISH**, **FRENCH**, Portuguese, Spanish.

However, the white minority, mostly the penchant and feebleminded Afrikaners, in order to perpetuate their power over the Black majority, started to practice apartheid. Apartheid simply means the official government practice of segregation in a society against certain races.

Many notable Black leaders had either been assassinated or imprisoned while protesting and/or trying to expurgate this anachronistic, immoral and dubious practice. Among the notables were Steven Biko who died under police custody from injuries to his head -- evidence of white police barbarism and brutality -- in 1977, and the most popular, of course, famous Nelson Rolihlahla Mandela serving a hasted and predetermined life sentence. Again, evidence of obstruction of justice. Born July 18, 1918, Mandela, a lawyer by educational training and civil rights and a political activist by choice, turned septuagenarian while still incarcerated. He remains a martyr, not only to South African Blacks, but all the freedom loving human race.

Several world leaders, including some conservative newspapers have called for his unconditional release. In its editorial of Sunday, July 24, 1988, titled NELSON MANDELA: South Africa Should Free Black Activist, The Dallas Morning News in Dallas, Texas, somewhat considered as a conservative newspaper, vehemently stated that, "For the first time the Reagan administration publicly has joined the world community in exhorting South Africa to free black nationalist leader Nelson Mandela. The leader of the African National Congress, who celebrated his 70th birthday last week in isolation, has been a political prisoner on South Africa's Robbin Island for more than 25 years."

"But even amidst growing international pressure," continued the paper, "Pretoria refused to waver in its insistence that it will not free Mr. Mandela until he renounces the use of violence.

"At first glance, the position may appear a legitimate response to a difficult political problem, but it fails to recognize intrinsic characteristics of the apartheid regime itself. One unsettling truth is that political violence in South Africa over the years has escalated as non-violent black efforts at democratic change have been crushed by the government, sometimes brutally.

"After all, where are many of the black South African leaders who have eschewed violence and advocated democratic change: In prison or dead. The world has not forgotten the tragic case of black activist leader Steve Biko, killed in custody in 1977. Mr. Biko was one of black South Africa's most charismatic symbols of non-violent black leadership. In contrast to the exile-based African National Congress, Mr. Biko also maintained a strong anti-Soviet stance. But none of these factors was sufficient in the minds of South African authorities to spare his life.

"It is becoming increasingly apparent," continued the newspaper, "that what the South African regime fears far more than the threat of violence is the threat of genuine political change, even if it is democratic. As early as 1964, the world learned what Mr. Mandela's true political values were when he stated at his trial, 'I have cherished the ideal of a democratic and free society in which all persons live together in harmony with equal opportunity'."

"The world," lamented the paper, "is now watching and waiting for Pretoria to demonstrate its true political values. The recent parliamentary debate on a bill claiming to expand the political role of the blacks who are the majority without giving them either the vote or genuine influence over their lives has far too little meaning to be perceived as progress. This is especially so when the same session of parliament decided to tighten rules on housing segregation.

"Pretoria finally must begin to act

in ways that can defuse the explosive environment of hostility apartheid has spawned. Freeing Nelson Mandela will be the first meaningful step in that process," the relatively conservative and maverick newspaper concluded.

The South African Blacks formed an authoritative party called the African National Congress (ANC) about January 8, 1912. In the beginning, they practiced non-violence protests as Mahatma Gandhi of India did during his days for his nation's independence, and as the late Reverend (Dr.) Martin Luther King, Jr. later carried on in the United States of America that eventually changed the conscience of the caucasians against the outrageous practice and tolerance of segregation, mildly dubbed as "separate but equal."

When this tenacious and excruciating non-violence practice yielded no sensitive soul among the white minority perpetrators and sympathizers, the ANC had no reasonable choice than to change tactics. Their initiation of violence was against their will, but it was the will of the time to extricate the constantly wronged people from the evil of apartheid.

Winnie Nomzamo Mandela, the wife of the nationalist leader wrongfully imprisoned "for life" by the apartheid regime in 1961 among others, for the so-called sabotage and subversion, otherwise known as treason, on Wednesday, August 22, 1985, said that her jailed husband, "Believes that the time has passed when South Africans of different races can settle their differences and chart the country's future through discussions at a national convention. The only other aspect that can be discussed by the people of this country and the ruling Afrikaners," she emphasized, "is the handing over of power."

The African National Congress had for long been outlawed in South Africa. Nonetheless, it is operated from Lusaka, The Zambian capital since the erroneous banishment.

That racist regime has outlawed almost every Black participation in protest of any kind. Thousands of children under puberty age had been detained for years without trial. Even organized church protest, other than mere prayer in the church, was equally banned. The Anglican Archbishop of the Southern African sub-continent, Dr. Desmond Tutu, also a Black South African, was detained at least once for organizing a religious protest of the cancerous apartheid. Archbishop Tutu was a Nobel Peace Laureate of 1984. Although Bishop Tutu has a South African passport, his citizenship, according to the passport, "will be determined at a future date."

Opposition newspapers, including those of churches, were banned. Neither Mandela, nor his wife Winnie, can be quoted in any form of media in South Africa. Reverend (Dr.) Allan Boesak had been detained and arm-bushed countless times. Every effort worth trying had been exerted by the racist government to torment the South African nationalists and freedom fighters. But God never sleeps.

It is believed that after the governance of South Africa rightfully goes back to the Black majority, the real indigenes of that present obscure nation, the country would be renamed AZANIA, as Zimbabwe genuinely replaced Rhodesia after independence in 1980.

Freedom does not come easily. In most cases, blood is usually spilled and heads rolled. As such, it must not be overlooked that other African nations, such as Nigeria, the self-designated giant of Africa, was once in the shoes the South African Blacks now found themselves.

This was reflected in a militant and uncompromising speech made by the president of the Zikist Movement, Raji Abdallah in 1949. (Zikist Movement was an organization formed on behalf of Dr. Nnamdi Benjamin Azikiwe of Nigeria shortly after he came back to Nigeria from Gold Coast, now Ghana, in 1937 to start or continue the struggle for Nigerian independence). Said Abdallah, "I hate the Union Jack with all my heart because it divides the people wherever it goes. We have passed the age of petition . . . the age of resolution . . . the age of diplomacy. This is the age of action -- plain, blunt, and positive action."

This speech made at the Glover Hall, Lagos, was considered seditious by the British (white) ruled government in Nigeria, as usual. The Zikist Movements were involved in various other activities, among which, it was alleged, included the involvement in the Enugu (capital of the defunct Eastern Region and during the civil war of Biafra) coal miners strikes of November 7, 1949, in which about 21 people lost their lives, and the February 18, 1950 assassination attempt of the Chief Secretary of the government, Mr. H. M. Foot by Heelas Ugokwe.

A surprise search at the houses of some of the "white" listed Zikists turned out "quantities of seditious literature." In a trial that ensued, it showed that the Zikists were adamant and uncompromising. The Movement was, on April 12, 1950, outlawed. Nigerians thereafter, with the help of the chain of events in the world then, coupled with the rejuvenated political awareness in Africa, embarked on other strategies, which eventually yielded fruitful results.

As it can be deduced, the South African Blacks' plights, which they are encountering today, were in one way or another suffered by their present liberated African brothers. A case in point was that of Algeria, which took several lives of her citizens in combatant effort with France before independence was achieved.

Nonetheless, the plights of Namibia, a supposedly independent nation that was a German colonial Territory, assigned as "mandate" to the Union of South Africa in 1919 by the League of Nations, now United Nations Organization, remain a nightmare to Africa. The United Nations, accordingly, had for long repealed the mandate it gave to the South African Government and authorized Namibia, also known as South West Africa, to be independent through Resolution 435.

However, the Republic of South Africa still illegally holds this de jure independent nation hostage against the will of the Namibians in particular and the world in general.

That was no wonder the Reverend Jesse Louis Jackson, the 1988 Black Democratic Presidential candidate in the United States of America, demanded that the Republic of South Africa, already ostracized by many nations, be declared a terrorist state in the Democratic Party platform of 1988 in that party's convention held in Atlanta, Georgia from Monday, July 18 to Thursday, July 21, 1988. He succeeded in his bold demand even though he lost the presidential nomination to Michael Stanley Dukakis who was at the time the able Governor of Massachusetts.

Dukakis, 55, to the dismay of many Black or African Americans who wanted Jesse Jackson to be at least his running mate, chose Texas Democratic conservative U. S. Senator Lloyd Bentsen. Senator Bentsen, 67 then, however, had a good civil rights record to his advantage. Dukakis, who was over a decade younger than Senator Bentsen, was rejected at the poll over Vice President George Herbert Walker Bush of the Republican Party on November 8, 1988. George Bush, irrespective of the mud-smearing campaign he ran, became the first sitting Vice President elected President in the U. S. since 1836. Bentsen who also ran for a Texas Senate seat was re-elected.

The South African racist government's linkage of Cuban troops in Angola as an excuse for the perpetration of its illegal acts in Namibia and Angola is reprehensible and is tantamount to unalloyed opprobrium.

It is paradoxical that the United

States of America, which preaches the gospel of democracy around the world, would, under Ronald Wilson Reagan, support the South African government's treacherous and pugnacious activities and its intentional destabilization of Black communities in the "Front Line" countries around her borders. The apartheid regime's practice of inundated fascism which leads to inanity is far much worse than any communist controlled government.

Still, the free world stands idly by to condone it. What happens to the simple freedom principle of self-determination? What happens to the political euphemism that "majority carries the vote?" President Reagan's government, all of a sudden, blatantly abandoned such cardinal principles of democracy. And in a propaganda ploy, it initiated "constructive engagement" with that disdainful regime of Pieter W. Botha.

The fate of Black South Africans and the Front Line States around the borders of this oblivious racist state is in the hands of Africans and the world at large. The second-class treatment of these loyal, dedicated, and illustrious sons and daughters of South Africa by the obdurated white minority government of Botha and his henchmen, coupled with the continuous illegal occupation and de facto control of Namibia are not only pathological and degrading to Africa, but an anathema to the world, the regime's romance with the Zulu chief, Gatsha Buthelezi and his Inkatha Movement notwithstanding.

This means that Africa is still struggling for its renascence, and must never rest until it is fully achieved, irrespective of the fact that Namibian independence is now slated for April 1, 1990 and Mandela more or less released from prison. (Mandela developed tuberculosis while in prison and was released to a secluded and guarded house where members of his family had no more visiting limitations.)

When the hagiology and/or hagiography of Neo-African nationalists and their sympathizers are written, those who had fallen in the battle or otherwise must not be forgotten.

Although the struggle for total emancipation of mankind rages on, unequal and subservient treatment of any race anywhere in the world, especially the disadvantaged or less powerful, must be execrated, and all necessary efforts exhausted to expurgate the odious situation.

It must not be forgotten, as the Bible reminds us, that all men are created equal by the same Omnipotent. And as man has come to realize, no condition is permanent. This illusion of life is among the mysteries that still bewilders mankind.

* * *

ECONOMIC INDEPENDENCE

Gaining political independence is one thing, economic independence is another. Unfortunately, most Africans were agriculturally oriented, particularly subsistence farming.

Said the analysis on Scramble for Africa by M. E. Chamberlain: "The influence of climate on civilization has fascinated both modern archaeologists and victorian scientists. Modern archaeologists would accept that favourable climate conditions helped the early emergence of relatively advanced human groups in Africa. The continent did not suffer the ravages of the Ice Age as Europe and Asia did. Its history was influenced rather by alternating 'wet' and 'dry' periods during which the size of the Sahara Desert varied greatly. In the 19th century, it was fashionable in some quarters to suppose that climatic conditions were decisive in determining relative degrees of civilization. Early anthropologists thought that all human society developed through three stages:

1. Savagery -- characterized by hunting and food-gathering;
2. Barbarism -- characterized by the emergence of settled agriculture; and
3. Civilization -- characterized by the development of commerce.

"To some Victorian observers," said the Analysis, "Africa seemed to have got stuck in the second stage. They sought explanations for this and found it was the doctrine of 'Tropical abundance'. The very richness of Africa had helped the progression from the first stage to the second but then tended to stultify progress because a tolerable life could be obtained with comparatively little effort. Advanced civilizations only appeared in temperate regions where a high degree of organization was necessary to ensure adequate food and shelter." The report, however, emphasized that "The inhabitants of all tropical regions, not just Africa, were likely to remain in this (second) stage," characterized by the emergence of settled agriculture.

Whether this report was as a result of the shock charge that Blacks were naturally "lazy" and always did the minimum of work, or out of tendentiousness of whiteman against Black Africans is debatable. However, it seems, as observed by P. D. Curtin in his "Image of Africa: British Ideas and Actions, 1780 - 1850," to have arisen partly because of the picture of the African "Negro," "drawn from the (often unfavourable) view that was held of the American slave, (and) partly because of a failure on the part of early observers to have any appreciation of the natural rhythms of work of any agrarian community."

Because of the unappreciation of the agrarian labour and effort, the raw materials were and still are exported at give-away prices in exchange for highly priced manufactured or finished foreign goods. This makes these African countries to depend much more on the developed world economically.

How was this ineptitude trend perpetuated to the chagrin of the Africans? When the whiteman came, he did not come as a "good samaritan" or santa claus. He came to exploit the people and their environs. To do that, they tried by all possible means to keep the indigenes virtually uneducated, to avoid opening their eyes to the ostensibly planned deprivation. The only education made available was the study of the English language, French, Portuguese or Spanish, purely for communication purposes.

African produce, mainly cash and food crops, were purchased at a slave-labour price. These cash crops were sent to Britain, France, Portugal, etc., to be used for finished products, which, of course, would in turn be sold to the Africans at cut-throat prices. Because the Europeans had the equipment and technical-know-how to transform the produce into a better appeal(l)ing goods, Africans were denied the access to the advanced knowledge. In the end, Africans became a dependent continent because of the snob-appeal they developed for foreign goods.

Whether this strategy was by omission, commission, or design, it worked for the Europeans. The situation became worse when Africans gained independence without much educated people to plan and execute the herculean tasks ahead. No institutions of higher learning to train the aborigines. Even those educated during the colonial era in mostly art subjects had to travel to the European home base in Britain, France, and what have you, to obtain the training. Consequently, African nations lacked many qualified engineers, economists, architects, doctors, lawyers, surveyors, accountants, to mention but a few, that would handle the now complex economy and brain-washed citizens. In some cases, the so-called colonial masters leave the economy virtually barren and empty before the hand over of power.

Nonetheless, most African nations could have broken away from this stigma of perverse cyclical poverty after about three decades or more of independence. After all, Japan, which was considered a third world country about two decades ago, now has emerged strongly technologically, out-competing even the giant nations like the United States of America. Japan which is relatively an island has no natural resources such as oil. Yet, with the spirit of discipline, nationalism, and dedication to work, it has assailed all odds and become an industrialized nation. But African countries have both human and natural resources in abundance; yet they lag behind. Is this due to lack of leadership, ineptitude, or lack of motivation?

The problems of African nations, however, are too enormous. Africa is a continent of too many races, tongues, and cultures. Any country of the world, such as the United States, which has only one language or a lingua-Franca must thank her stars. With the exception of Tanzania, under Honorable Dr. Julius Nyerere, which has one national language, Swahili, used in the parliament as opposed to the English language, African countries are split on tribalism. People tend to be more loyal to their tribe than to the nation.

Wrote one Dan Agbese about Dr. Nnamdi Azikiwe of Nigeria, "Perhaps, politics in every land where tribal loyalties override national loyalties needs a beautiful bride" like Zik. This tribal issue is a major problem in Africa.

However, if lack of education and tribalism alone are the problems, it could be better. But greediness, overzealousness and individualism, as opposed to collectivism, tolerance, understanding and national interest make things worse.

Politics becomes a means for financial self-enrichment instead of national service and sacrifice. Politics is no more the art of the possible, but a forum for irreconcilable antagonism. Accountability becomes a foreign diction.

In a discussion with Edward Gargan of the New York Times News Service that appeared in The Dallas Morning News in Texas on Thursday, October 3, 1985, Dr. Doyin Okupe, a senior physician at Royal Cross Hospital, Lagos, the "old" capital of Nigeria, lamented thus: "The thing that we do not have in this part of the world is sincerity of purpose. In this country, we do not do anything for posterity. In this country, poverty is not very far from us.

"There is a tendency for someone who has not seen much money before to try and amass as much wealth as possible. This desire has led to corruption. This unfortunately happens in all Africa. It appears to me that the idea of democracy is alien to African culture. Look at Zimbabwe where Mugabe is moving to a one-party state. Look at the Ivory Coast, Togo."

With an astonishing sigh, he concluded, "These countries in Africa are very young. It does in a way have to do with the age of a country." Does it?

What about Chile which had her independence on September 18, 1818, Philippines with independence on June 12, 1898, Mexico with independence on September 16, 1810, Panama with independence on November 3, 1903, Haiti with independence since January 1, 1804, and Iran, formerly Persia, though invaded several times, but had not actually been colonized.

All these are old countries in different continents. Smaller and relatively young countries like Taiwan, South Korea, to mention but just two, are considerably economically buoyant and politically stable than the so-called old countries. Come to think about it, it does not have much to do with race or age of a country; it has to do with greed and gullibility of man, culminating on the fact that man is insatiable in his quest for wealth and power. This is the residue of archaic systems that lack adequate checks and balances.

Experts in the epistemology of nations would agree that the age of a country does not necessarily matter much in planning for the future and fate of a nation. The people matter. The charismatic and visionary ability to lead for the benevolence of the common man matter much more.

Haiti, a Central American nation which is the oldest black independent country in the world after Ethiopia, is still in search of political and economic viability. In a revolt by the people of that country with a tacit help from the United States of America, the country's dictator, Jean-Claude Duvalier who bestowed upon himself "president-for-life" was forced to abdicate his power and flee the country on February 7, 1986. His father, Dr. Francois Duvalier, was elected to office in 1957, but in 1964, he enshrined himself "president-for-life." His son, Jean-Claude, became president of Haiti in 1971 at the age of 19 after his father departed this world in peace, perhaps to Hades. Like his father, he made a maximum use of the underground police called Tonton Macoutes to suppress and exterminate opposition.

Nonetheless, after Duvalier and his family left for exile in France, a three-man Provisional Council was set up as a transition to democratic rule. It was headed by Lt. General Henri Namphy until a legitimate election of civilian government was conducted.

The election was set for November 29, 1987. What happened next? On the day of the election, the military covertly aided the Tonton Macoutes which did not want an election to be held, simply because the adopted new national constitution barred anybody associated with the Duvalier family, either in kinship or administration, from participating in any election for 10 years. About 200 electioneerers, including some presidential candidates, were reported either murdered or missing on or about the election day. Thousands, of course, were injured. It was horrible.

In Port-au-Prince, the capital, people were running helter skelter for their life. Of course, the military junta had an excuse to cancel the election. Even before the election, Henri Namphy had promulgated a decree naming himself Chief of Army Staff for several years after the civilian government might have assumed power. Any African who had witnessed coup d' etat, most probably would know what was behind the idea. The civilian government would have been a puppet regime, just like what happened in Panama under General Manuel Antonio Noriega as the Army Chief of Staff. The election, however, was rescheduled two months later after Lt.

Gen. Namphy fired the Constituted Electoral Commission and set up his own, in flagrant defiance of the new constitution which he signed into law.

On the day of the so-called second election attempt, January 17, 1988, less than 15% of the eligible electoral voters went to the poll, not only as a protest to the proposed sham election, but for fear of similar terror of two months earlier. This facsimile and apparent fraudulent election, an act of the military, in part showed that the age of a country is not the problem. Diminished selfless service, coupled with careless planning of a nation's future are the problems.

Leslie Manigat, a former political science professor who was in exile during Duvalier's dictatorial era, won the support of Namphy and Brig. General Williams Regala, and subsequently won the executive presidency. Due to an insubordination on the part of Namphy who enacted a decree and transferred officers without the president's permission or consent, Manigat exercised what he thought was his executive privilege and retired him (Namphy) on June 17, 1988. For security purposes, he ordered him under house arrest. He rescinded the orders originally given by Namphy.

On the morning of Monday, June 20, 1988, Namphy supporters broke the arrest, helped him to stage a successful coup which sent Manigat back to another exile, this time to the Dominican Republic.

Col. Jean-Claude Paul whom President Leslie Manigat was counting on for assistance could not help him retain his power. Col. Paul, arrogantly indicted by the U.S. government for drug charges but headed the best equipped Infantry Battalion in Haiti was among the soldiers Namphy demoted and transferred. Although Manigat overruled Namphy in keeping him, neither he, nor his command unit could overcome the determination and toughness of Namphy's loyalists.

To avoid a counter coup that might bring back Prof. Manigat to power, Namphy rewarded Paul by letting him keep his envious command unit. This move made some political analysts think that Manigat was deceitfully lured into conflict with the army. But Namphy's plan did not seat well with the non-commissioned officers. Tired of the anarchy and the government's arrogance of power, especially its inaction on the murder of the Catholic Churchgoers in August and September, 1988, by Tonton Macoutes, the sergeants deposed Namphy and gave the reign of powers to Maj. Gen. (later Lt. Gen.) Prosper Avril on September 17, 1988. Namphy, like Manigat was sent to the Dominican Republic on exile. But Jean-Claude Paul, 49, whom Avril retired by force out of fear, was food-poisoned to death on Sunday, November 6, 1988. Some people are pointing accusing fingers at the United States CIA whose country indicted Col. Paul, in collusion with Col. Paul's wife who allegedly gave him the poisoned soup he ate that Sunday. The wife initially claimed that it was a heart attack that killed the able soldier.

The Time Magazine (in U.S.A.) of December 21, 1987, posed thus: "Will Africa, fabulously rich in natural resources, ever end the cycle of war, disease and over population that helps to keep it poor and famished?" It went on to say that "Most African governments, including those much less radical than Ethiopia, continue to be wedded to quasi-socialist, postcolonial economic policies that reduce agricultural productivity, even as populations soar and create voracious demand for more food."

The economic system of most African nations is hard to categorize. In some instances, their economies defy established economic theories. They cannot be crystalized as a capitalist, communist, or socialist economic system. This is agonizing indeed.

However, in fairness, it may be called a mixed economy, but with great leaning towards socialism. The government controls almost every major sector of the economy, such as electricity, telephone, most transportation systems, schools, hospitals, the media, including the major newspapers, radio and television network, to mention just a few instances.

In some countries, the one-party system of politics is practiced. There is little or no checks and balances in their government operational horizon. Without supervision by one branch of the government over the other, how can there be accountability and serenity, which in turn could lead to progress. Consequently, any improvement in research and development are stagnated.

The general public rarely has any recourse. All these compound and exacerbate the chronic and perverse cyclical economic down turn and the resultant poverty in Africa.

The economic planning which is barely executed is hardly evaluated. As a matter of fact, implementation is the centre of African leaders' fallibility and imbecility. In most cases, political appointment of cronies and family members take precedent over long-term national interest. The implication of this is that nepotism and tribalism can never be eliminated in toto in the African economic and political life. And the nemesis is the constant insurgency and never ending rebellion in that continent.

Even the Union of Soviet Socialist Republics (U.S.S.R.), otherwise known as Russia, through its General Secretary (leader) Mikhail Sergeyevich Gorbachev, has revolutionalized and polished its communist system. (Gorbachev's title became President in early October 1988.)

Through his book titled, PERESTROIKA: NEW THINKING FOR OUR COUNTRY AND THE WORLD, Gorbachev told the world how he wanted to reform his country's fledgling economy. He said that Perestroika (restructuring) is a revolution. Quite a revolution from Karl Marx's ideology of communism. He admitted though, that it proved more difficult than they had at first imagined, and "We have had to reassess many things. Revolution requires the demolition of all that is obsolete, stagnant and hinders fast progress. Without demolition, you cannot clear the site for new construction. Perestroika also means a resolute and radical elimination of obstacles hindering social and economic development, of outdated methods of managing the economy. Perestroika," he continued, " affects the interest of the whole society. And, of course, demolition provokes conflicts and sometimes fierce clashes between the old and the new. There are no bombs exploding or bullets flying, but those who are in the way resist. And inaction, indifference, laziness, irresponsibility and mismanagement are also resistance," he wrote.

Gorbachev also pointed out in his book that politics is the art of the possible. And beyond the limits of the possible begins adventurism.

If the Soviet Union, a symbol of communism can see some inefficiency in the socialist system and work toward its reformation, why can't African nations, which are neither pure socialist, nor pure capitalist, reform and religiously reevaluate their economy. As a matter of fact, there is nothing like pure capitalist or pure communist systems in the present day complex economy. Countries have gradually reformed toward each other's school of thought.

The gargantuan of the African problem is mostly lack of motivation for self-development and awareness. Everybody wants to get rich quick without toiling for it. The Kakki boys want to overthrow the mandated civilian government to have their own share of the national cake. The traders want to import finished products instead of manufacturing them at home, because it is easier to import (them) than go through the rigour of planning, designing and execution before thinking of remuneration. The local contractors want to defraud the government by doing little or nothing for the contractual fees paid. The people on the seat of power equally award infrastructural contracts to foreign firms for a gentleman's agreement of a certain percentage bribe which is often paid into secret Swiss or British bank accounts.

Said the Newswatch Board of Economics as reported by Newswatch of December 21, 1987 on foreign contracts in Nigeria, "European firms mainly and some American firms just move for the kill. They even go so far as to have special prices for Nigeria. That is why the cost of contracts in Nigeria is higher than any other African country. For instance, the Murtala Muhammed (International) Airport, Ikeja cost about three times more than a similar one in Kenya, the Jomo Kenyatta Airport. Foreigners in our midst have done a lot of harm, but they could not do it without the active support and collaboration of Nigerians." The Board went on to say, with authority, that some leading Nigerian industrialists and chairmen of big firms are merely the errand boys for foreign firms. "Their main function is to sort out difficulties in award or payment of contracts executed. The foreign firms know how these public relations functions are performed." Therefore, the Board said, "When they quote for contract projects, they build the cost of public relations into the price."

This allegation is no exaggeration. It is even very subtle to what is prevailing, not only in Nigeria, but in Africa all over. And that is the reason when the project is not properly executed, there are no questions asked, because, the officer in charge of overseeing the project got his own share of the (expended) procurement.

The motto of the famous Dick Tiger Memorial Secondary School in Amaigbo, Orlu, in Imo State, Nigeria, is "Destiny in our hands." During those secondary school days, one did not know, nor did one care about such dictum. But as it turns out, everyone carries his own cross, and Africa, as a continent, is no exception. The destiny of Africa is in the hands of Africans. It is very disheartening that the flounder of one African affects the integrity of all Africans. The world sees the blunder of one African nation as the imbroglio and imbecility of all Africans. In the United States of America, when the victims of famine in Ethiopia were shown in 1984, 1985 and early 1986, they were shown as Africans and not as Ethiopians. But again, the Ethiopian government was engaged in an unnecessary and indignified civil war with its northern provinces citizens, namely Tigre (or Tigray) and Eritrea provinces. The resources that could be used to save the famine victims were plunged in armament. Over one million Ethiopians reportedly died of starvation between 1984 and early 1986 in one of the worst droughts in the African continent, before the world, after dissipated politicking, came to the mellowed rescue.

Bob Geldof who championed a relief effort in London with his "Band Aid" which raised millions of pounds to help the dying Ethiopians, during his revisitation to Ethiopia in 1987, chastised the Lt. Col. Mengistu Haile Mariam administration. He charged the government of fighting "ideological battles over the heads of dying people." He lamented, "I think it is the cardinal responsibility of any government to be able to feed its people." On the rebels, he said, "To attack food trucks and seal off roads in these conditions is tantamount to mass murder." If Ethiopia was at peace, couldn't the government have foreseen the roaming drought? Or would it subject her citizens to the impending peril? As the starvation was taking more lives than the battle field, was it not symbiotically ingenious to fight the hunger and/or the drought than ideological differences? What happens to the ingenuity of compromise? Perhaps, if the fund for ammunition was channelled into irrigation system of agriculture, this catastrophe could have been minimized. This kind of asininity is not peculiar with Ethiopia; it is axiomatic with the third world's political operation. Thank God that peace is relatively back to that country after Haile Mariam, who is now the President of

Ethiopia, proposed a confederation in September, 1988, which may now give the rebellious provinces an autonomous power they had longed for since.

To date, Africa continues to lag behind economically. To be fully independent, a country or continent in this case, must be economically buoyant, other things being equal. Otherwise the developed nations in a strong footing would be dictating the way she plans and operates, and the future would remain uncertain.

As stated eloquently and unequivocally by this author in his book titled THE AGONY: THE UNTOLD TALE OF THE NIGERIAN SOCIETY, it reads, "For any country to advance economically and technologically, three major factors must be present:

1. *There must be available resources from which the development will be implemented.*

2. *There must be political stability that would foster and encourage the development to take place, including inflow of capital.*

3. *There must be willingness on the people to accept a change.*"

Even Dr. George Pratt Shutz, a U. S. A. Secretary of State during Ronald

Reagan's two consecutive terms, in a speech to the Senegalese Business Council delivered at the Central Bank for West African States on Thursday, January 8, 1987, recognized the African problems. Said he, "There are untapped savings in (African Continent) traditional market systems. There is a wealth of entrepreneurial talent waiting for the right incentives. If the energies of the African peoples can be liberated for productive enterprise, and I'm confident they can, then our long-term reform effort . . . will know success."

One couldn't have agreed any further that there is "a wealth of entrepreneurial talent awaiting for the right incentive" in Africa. Africans have the resources. The problem is the lack of direction of purpose and unpoliticized motivation which in the end would lead to economic and political stability. Convincing the citizens to accept positive change would initially meet resistance but would eventually be well received. The unalienable responsibility to lead positively, decisively and unbiasedly rests with the oligarchical enclave called rulers. The Wall Street Journal in the U.S.A. in late 1983 stated that, "Two decades after the continent claimed its independence, Africa is in political despair. Strongmen reign, armies rule, civil liberties are luxury that its rulers say Africa cannot afford."

Nonetheless, in some African countries, "Fisher effect" is what is in operation. The government in some cases would adopt a relatively genuine and good policy, but the gluttonous citizens would thwart the effort by taking the advantage of any loop-hole. This in turn would force the penchant and distensible government to adopt stricter and more radical policies. The strictness, depending on how far the government is forced to go, could lead to fascism, which in its face, is dictatorship, assuming other checks and balances are watered down.

It is very imperative for Africans to think about the future. The government cannot do it alone without the absolute or honest cooperation of the citizens. The citizens have to redirect their government from time to time. This is a civic duty. They have the right to have free and independent press to monitor what is "cooking" in the seat of authority. Fear of exposure most of the time forces the leaders to be honest with their work, or at least to be logical. It must be understood that absolute power corrupts absolutely. But to blow the whistle against an incumbent takes courageous press. The price paid most of the time is very costly, but at the end, it is worth it, especially if the castigated and maltreated honest journalist or whistle-blower is venerated by the understanding public.

Newswatch Magazine in Nigeria, barring any change in style, comes into the picture at this juncture. One of its founders, Dele Giwa, educated in the United States of America and well known in the journalism industry in Nigeria for his outspokenness against any corrupt regime in Nigeria, be it military or civilian government, was murdered in cold blood with a lethal time bomb alleged to have been given to him by the State Security Service (SSS) agent through the auspices of the Military Intelligence. He died as a result of the explosion on October 19, 1986. His associates carried on. Under the leadership of Ray Ekpu who became the Editor-in-Chief and CEO after the death of Giwa, the magazine was, six months later, proscribed on April 6, 1987, for six months. Reason: It "prematurely" published the report of the political bureau on the transition to civil rule. The government charged that the report was obtained illegally and that its publication violated the official secrets act. On the second anniversary of the regime's assumption of power, August 27, 1987, the ban was lifted.

With the irony of fate, six months after the magazine came back to life, it was selected, and later honoured by the World Press Review, a non-profit organization based in New York, U.S.A., for "Courage" and excellence in journalism based on the magazine's article about Mikhail Gorbachev in 1987. The award to the Chief Editor, who was accompanied by many dignitaries in Nigeria, was received on May 10, 1988 in New York. The selection of Newswatch over all world magazines was not unconnected with its turbulence with the Nigerian government since its existence from January 28, 1985. During the ban on the magazine, its top officials were arrested and detained for at least one day. They were later released without charges.

The major setback in the economic reform in Africa hinges on the inability of the iconoclasts to convince, persuade and/or force the power-mongers in Africa to practice laissez-faire economic system, by allowing the law of "invisible hands" to operate, at least to a moderate degree. Adam Smith, through his "Wealth of Nations" published in 1776, propounded this idea. With little government intrusion or moderation, the theory of "let demand and supply shape the course of the market" or economy still makes sense. If Africans could let this law of demand and supply, of course, with government intervention where it is absolutely necessary as Neo (John Maynard) Keynesians would agree, the economy of Africa would rebound at a geometric progression. It might not be easy at first. But with the passage of time, it will come at the equilibrium point where all sides of the market will be satisfied.

Economists agree that at the long run, all capital becomes variable. Prices of the output, in the beginning will be costly because producers would try to maximize profit to reduce their initial, and perhaps patent costs. This attracts competitors and efficient production; hence, eventual price slashes.

This author is not a fan of David A. Stockman, a former U. S. congressman and former conservative Budget Director of the Ronald Reagan White House in the United States of America. But his comment in his controversial book titled, "The Triumph of Politics: Why the Reagan Revolution Failed," published in 1986 makes some sense. He noted that "What liberals have never been able to bring themselves to admit is that capitalism is the product of capitalists. It is the prospect of getting rich and keeping the rewards that drives invention, innovation, and entrepreneurial risk taking."

Government-monopolized corporations in Africa lack competition. Without competition, there would rarely be invention and/or innovation. The resultant outcome is inefficiency. The argument for governments is that if individuals are left to run certain industries like electricity, air line, telephone, post and telegraphs, etc., that the price will be too high for the average person to bear. It is true that in the beginning the price will be high as stated earlier, because of the fixed capital investment in the initial production. But as the company eventually makes profits and other people or companies are attracted to compete, the forces of demand and supply will come to work. To the benefit of the final consumer, time is saved; bribery that would be given to the government employees according to their hierarchy when the government alone was doing it would be eliminated; taxes are paid by these companies out of profits made; and above all, efficiency is restored.

The initial "third" world governments' involvement in the operation of "commercial" activities, particularly after their independence, was justified on the ground that their citizens did not have enough (capital) resources to operate such giant ventures like Air Lines, Electricity, Television/Radio network, domestic transportation, telephone, Universities, etc.

But as their citizens become economically able to invest and venture risks, governments need to give them a chance to compete, not only to increase efficiency, but to invent and innovate new technology for the betterment of the citizens, governments, and mankind.

Rather, these governments and the leaders stuck to the old ideas. No changes. They use political appointments to those government parastatals which were supposed to be temporary (moves), as political weapons and intimidation against the citizens they are supposed to serve effectively and to their best interest. Thus, corruption persists.

In the United States of America and most developed nations, companies compete on both local and long distance telephone lines. The American Telephone and Telegraph (AT&T) is not owned by any government, nor G.T.E., I.T.T. (International Telephone and Telegraph) or Sprint. Even Southwestern Bell, named after Alexander Graham Bell (1847-1922), the inventor of the telephone, which handles most local and some limited long distance calls in the U.S., is not government owned either.

It might be necessary to take you on a short trip to Nigeria, in West Africa, to dramatize the efficiency of laissez-faire system when applied. Shortly after the end of the Biafran-Nigerian civil war in January, 1970, Bendel State of Nigeria, under the governorship of Brigadier Samuel Ogbemudia (now retired), started running luxury Bendel Line transport system. The system was relatively modeled like Trailways or Greyhound in the United States. The price then was about twenty Naira from Lagos to Imo State. Shortly after, EKENE DI LI CHUKWU transport (private enterprise) came in, as well as Iyang Ete transport. Competition kicked off.

Talking about competition, Osondu transport, Chidi Ebele, Ifesinachi, The Young Shall Grow, to mention but a few, all incorporated transport services, came into the arena. The fare dropped precipitously to eight Naira. The government owned Bendel Line was run out of business in about three years. All the other transport companies mentioned above survived, including some new entrants, and transport fare is still comparatively low.

Also think about the state owned Nigeria Airways which had been in the red even though it had no domestic competitor. When Okada Air owned by Chief Gabriel Igbinedion was granted a charter to operate only local flights in 1982, the first time an individual was allowed to crack the wall of monopoly of the air line industry in Nigeria, what happened? In Okada Air, there is no bribery. It is pay and board; first come, first served. The Okada Air started with only one air plane. By 1987, it had more than 14 fleets. It virtually ran the Nigeria Airways out of the routes it once dominated. The

Airways complained bitterly so that the government could rescind the Okada charter, but to no avail. Okada Air, in late 1988, was granted an international charter by the Nigerian government in those areas Nigeria Airways was pulled out due to financial losses.

In the Nigeria Airways, employees hardly give good service; not even an early courtesy notice that the air line departure was being delayed. Not even an apology for any inconveniences. They hardly sell drinks in their own currency. They expect dollars or pounds sterling instead. On top of that, they expect a bribe or kick-back before rendering their service, which otherwise had been paid for under normal course of business system.

The Chairman of Nigeria Airways had always been a political appointee with little or no knowledge about the airline business or business in general. Imagine that. They forget, as one American president once said, that "American business is business." The military government of General Ibrahim B. Babangida, in July 1988, promulgated a decree 25 which included 60% privatization of the Nigeria Airways. But the airline was about two billion Naira in debt both locally and internationally. Two of its fleets were seized in France around May 1988 for the debt it owed when the planes were sent for maintenance. Did someone just say, what a shame?

The debt obviously discourages private investment. The best bet among many is that the government would liquidate the air line, and probably help found another one. But meanwhile, the British Airways which just acquired the British Caledonian took virtual monopoly and exercise of arrogance against the Nigerian travellers. At their urging, flight fare tripled.

Why shouldn't the private concerns run the television network or compete with the government network in African nations? The so-called leaders, or should they be called the privileged few, have the fear of illusion that the security of their nations could be compromised. What security? Is it the security of nuclear magnetic resonance or of exposing their ill-gotten wealth?

While the majority of the citizens in this continent are languishing in chagrin and squalor, the ruling few are siphoning the meagre "national cake" to a foreign economy. The Parade Magazine in the U.S.A. once carried an intelligence news report in the early 1980s that about $50 billion in Swiss banks belong to the unnamed accounts. It further stressed that most of the owners of the accounts were leaders of some "impoverished African nations." This allegation seems to have validity, especially as a finger is being pointed at Mobutu Sese Seko of Zaire of stuffing about $4 billion in Swiss banks while his nation languished in poverty. This is an evidence of absolute power and corruption. Mobutu exercises absolute power in his country.

This kind of leakage from the national treasury and/or foreign reserves does not only stifle a nation's economic growth and prosperity, it crumbles any future economic planning, implementation and revival. What African nations need is financial injection and not leakages from the dwindling economy. If the looted funds are reinvested, it could create a multiplier effect that in the long run may reinvigorate the economy and lead it to the way of buoyancy.

Most African leaders, like most other third world leaders, have money in foreign banks that is more than the loan they constantly beg from the International Monetary Fund (IMF) or World Bank in the name of their "broke" countries. Most of the time, when they die, the money is gone forever since only they know the secret codes to those accounts.

As it can be seen now, it is not only an African problem; it is also both developing and developed world problems. For example, the deposed Philippine dictator, Ferdinand Marcos, had millions of dollars in Swiss and U.S. banks while the economy of his country which he swore to protect was crumbling to a halt. Luckily for the Filipinos, he was ousted by Mrs. Corazon Aquino (the wife of his arch political foe, Sen. Benigno Aquino, Jr., who was gunned down on arrival from exile in the U.S.A. at the Manila Airport by a Marcos loyalist, allegedly at Marcos' order, on August 21, 1983) and her "people power" who defeated him on February 7, 1986 election, even though he insisted to be in power. He finally fled into exile (to Hawaii, U.S.A.) on February 25, 1986. Thereafter, his ill-gotten treasure he sucked from the poor people was exposed. The Swiss authorities and judiciary decided to cooperate with the Aquino government, at its request, to recover the money. In fact, Imelda Marcos, his wife, had over 3,000 pairs of shoes. This was discovered after they fled to the U.S.A.

Filipinos were inadvertently blessed that Marcos was not succeeded by one of his cronies; otherwise, they could have been subjected to the same squalidness and unabated discomfiture. In June 1988, a Swiss judge ordered one of the banks that Marcos had an account with, to return over $47 million to the Philippine government without delay. What a victory for the poor country. The government is still fighting for the repatriation of other hundreds of millions of dollars in both U.S.A. and Switzerland banks.

According to the Los Angeles Times of July 26, 1988, "Former Philippine President Ferdinand Marcos has offered to give back $5 billion and to support the government of President Aquino if he is permitted to return home without criminal prosecution. Marcos' representatives are now making an effort to avert his indictment in the United States by promising U.S. officials that he will, for the first time, promote 'national reconciliation' in the Philippine", the paper said. The paper went on to elaborate that his representatives "have entered into talks with Philippine officials including Philippine Ambassador to the United States, Emmanuel Pelaez--seeking a deal in which Marcos would pay $5 billion for the right to return to his home province of Ilocos Norte, according to political science Professor A. James Gregor of the University of California at Berkeley" who had been in contact with both parties.

When Marcos was contacted that same day, he confirmed that a deal was in the making but described the amount mentioned as ridiculous. Now who knows for sure how much he (actually) embezzled. Marcos and his wife, Imelda, however, were indicted in the U.S. on Friday, October 21, 1988 for fraud involving millions of dollars.

The six-count, 79-page indictment

accused the Marcoses of stealing $103 million in Philippine government funds through embezzlement, bribes, theft and kickbacks between 1972 and 1986, when they fled their country to seek sanctuary in Hawaii, U.S.A. The money, in addition to $165 million in loans they fraudulently obtained from three U.S.A. banks, was used to buy art and four office buildings in exclusive sections of New York, the indictment documents charged.

Said James Fox, Assistant Director of the Federal Bureau of Investigation (FBI), the Marcoses were "using their position of trust to turn Philippine treasury into their personal treasury. When they decided they wanted to own a piece of the rock, that piece of the rock became real estate in Manhattan," New York. Among those indicted with the Marcoses were Saudi arms dealer Adnan Khashoggi who used to be the world's richest man, and Marcos' former ambassador to the Vatican City.

Unlike Britain, and sometimes France which provided safe haven to the corrupt African and third world's fugitives, the U.S. was courageous enough to indict its former ally. Britain was reluctant to prosecute and/or extradite those corrupt fellows, particularly the Nigerian politicians, such as Umaru Dikko, Adisa Akinloye, etc. who fled their country in Janaury 1984 with millions of dollars to seek santuary there. France did nothing in the case of "Baby Doc" Duvalier of Haiti who fled his country on February 7, 1986.

African leaders, while fighting for their political survival, must not forget the overriding issue of their country-- ECONOMY. An African hardly succumbs to a defeat in Africa. But in a game like politics, it is either one wins or one loses. If one has the zeal to run, why shouldn't one muster courage to accept defeat likewise.

The long term benefit of all citizens of any nation must supersede any selfish interest or ambition of any person. Although the world is now interdependent, the more economically buoyant a nation is, the more real independent it becomes. The reason for this assertion is that politics and economy are inter-twined.

As an Igbo aphorism has it, "*Onye ebe ya na agba oku, anaghi achu oke*", literally meaning that one whose house is on fire, does not pursue rat. Mikhail Gorbachev summed this adage up succinctly when he told the Central Committee of the Soviet Politburo shortly before he became the General-Secretary (Head) of Soviet Union in 1985 that, "We cannot remain a major world power in world affairs unless we put our domestic house in order."

In African case, they cannot have a quantum of world influence until they eliminate or minimize their acrimonious behaviour against each other, strive to contain the abject poverty that befell the innocent citizens due to the maladministration and corruption of certain enclave, and plan for the future and welfare of the posterity.

PART TWO

* * *

COUP D' ETAT IN AFRICA

The main reason generally cited that necessitates the chronic political unrest, otherwise known as coup d' etat in Africa, is the unaccountability of the elected or self-installed leaders.

However, it could be logically argued that it is due to absolute power mania of the soldiers that bring them into political arena too. After all, it has been the easiest way of ascending into the nation's highest office.

The charge becomes more credible if one puts into consideration the view of the so-called distinguished colonial administrator, Sir Bartle Frere, with a wide experience of India, as well as Africa during early 19th century as depicted by H. A. C. Cairns in the book, Prelude to Imperialism: British Reactions to Central African Society, 1840-1890, published in Routledge in 1965.

Frere, according to the book, said that "If you read the history of any part of the Negro population of Africa, you will find nothing but a dreary recurrence of tribal wars, and an absence of everything which forms a stable government, and year after year, generation after generation, century after century, these tribes go on obeying no law but that of force, and consequently never emerging from the state of barbarism in which we find them at present, and in which they have lived, so far as we know, for a period long anterior to our own."

Nonetheless, the behaviour of the politicians themselves and the resulting concern of the general public as the major cause of military infringement in the socio-political process in Africa, cannot be unequivocally ruled out.

The "Renascent Africa," as Dr. Nnamdi Azikiwe, along with his African nationalist colleagues foresaw it, never came to pass. At least not yet. The mundane greed of man engulfed every decency and enormity of just, equitable, and honest governance.

Dr. Azikiwe, now an octogenarian, statesman and father of the nation (Nigeria), in his book titled Renascent Africa, published in 1937, saw Africa as "rising again into vigour," as it was emerging from the colonial tutelage to freedom. By Zik's definition, a renascent Africa must be spiritually balanced, socially regenerated, economically deterministic, mentally emancipated, and politically resurgent.

In a country where everybody was in chains, wrote Ray Ekpu on November 23, 1987, liberation was the battle cry and it was fitting for any writer at the time to devote attention to the subject of the moment.

What was said during the struggle for independence though, was obviously different from what was whispered after the mantle and gavel have been returned to the rightful, unalienable owners. The independent Africa of today, based on their political unrest and economic and technological stagnation can attest to that.

In many African countries, there is no true democracy. Many of the countries are ruled by one-party system of government. Any opposition is usually crushed. As a result, people are afraid to dissent. Any dissension, of course, would not only be the political demise of the person's ambition, but the extermination of himself from the face of this earth. Then, what is the difference between one-party state and despotic governance. There might be some mystifying difference, but the little variation in between in favour of one-party system may be so microscopic that it renders the chunk invalid. Well, let the political scholars dribble with that.

However, an example of a deplorable one-party state of government can be drawn from Liberia with capital in Monrovia.

William Vacanarat Shadrach Tubman was the Liberian president from January 1, 1944 till his death in July 1971. His Vice-President for about 28 years, William R. Tolbert, took over as president under the same party platform.

In 1975, he was elected President for an 8-year term beginning in January 1976. Almost all the members of Tolbert's family held key positions in the government. It was estimated that more than half of the assets in Liberia belonged to Tolbert's family. He was unable to reform the country to benefit the common man.

This led to his assassination and that of other cabinet members in a bloody coup d'etat of April 12, 1980, under the leadership of Master-Sergeant Samuel K. Doe. Sergeant Doe (later General) exposed what had been a secret for a long time. He tried as much as he could to reform the oligarchic system. He encountered some resistance from some of the people who found the existing condition satisfactory, and as expected, from foreign exploiters. Under his auspices, the archaic constitution of the country handed over to them after their liberation from slavery in 1844, was changed.

There was an assassination attempt on Doe in April 1985 that substantially marred the proposed return to civilian rule. On November 12, 1985, ex-general Thomas Quiwonkpa who was allowed to return from exile, launched an abortive coup against Gen. Doe's regime. Quiwonkpa was killed in that attempt. In the civilian election that was eventually held, featuring Gen. Doe as one of the candidates, came to pass. Doe claimed victory on the face of the flying allegations that he rigged the election to his favour. He was, nevertheless, formally sworn in as President on January 6, 1986. Perhaps to preempt what the U. S. did to Gen. Manuel Antonio Noriega of Panama, he changed his country's currency from dollar to his name -- Doe currency. The money was all coins; no paper money. This alienated him further from the businessmen who thought that they would become easy prey to armed robbers.

President Doe relatively invent innovative ideas but he surrounded himself with people of mediocrity. It is believed within Liberia that because he was barely educated, he became suspicious of the elites who could effectively implement his programmes. He has survived some attempted coups, including the one on Tuesday, July 12, 1988 by Gen. Nicholas Podier, his former associate in the People's Redemption Council whom he retired. Podier was killed during the cross fire.

The reason behind the minting of only coins as opposed to printing notes as currency was to deter, not only immediate flight of capital, but to prevent the sale of Liberian currency abroad -- a shame some of her neighbours, particularly Nigeria, suffered between 1982 and 1984.

The economy of Liberia has worsened though, and the unemployment rate is high. If he would turn the economy around as he strongly hoped, those who had been calling for his ouster might have change of heart. The problem with the economy was not all of his own making. The U. S. assistantship used to be a great portion of their national budget. But U. S. which did not like Doe's radical ideas, cut off most aids. If his people would understand his plights, it is believed that Doe can salvage the economic problems and still hold his head high. But some want a piece of him as he continued his arrogance and "immaturity."

Nigeria, among other African countries has had the same or similar fate as Liberia. Nigeria which had its independence on October 1, 1960, was militarily overthrown by a bloody coup d'etat on January 15, 1966 when Dr.

Nnamdi Azikiwe was the president and Alhaji Abubakar Tafawa Balewa, the prime minister. Only Azikiwe luckily escaped the wrath of death, simply because, or at least it seemed, he was on medical treatment abroad during the coup.

Although Nigeria did not have one-party state, it did have three-party system aligned to her three major tribes -- Action Group (AG) for Yoruba, National Council of Nigeria and Cameroon, later National Council of Nigerian Citizens (NCNC) for the Ibos, and Northern People's Congress (NPC) for the Hausas. Because of the political polarization and unrest that ensued shortly after the head of the Action Group, now late Chief Obafemi Awolowo and his deputy, Chief Anthony Enahoro, who had escaped to Britain but extradited on May 16, 1963, were sentenced to 10 years and 15 years on September 11, and September 7, 1963 respectively, for treason, on their conspiracy to overthrow the Federal Government of Nigeria by force, and some inaction on corruption of the public officials, the army staged a coup.

Major Chukwuma Kaduna Nzeogwu led the coup d'etat of the (5) majors. However, Major-General Johnson Thomas Umunnakwe Aguiyi-Ironsi, the highest ranking indigenous army official in Nigeria and West Africa, a typical army veteran who rose through the ranks tightly controlled by the British, was given the honour to lead the nation by the coup lords, after some negotiations and concessions from Gen. Ironsi. Major Nzeogwu's agreement with Ironsi, which led to the surrender of his sword, among other things, included a guarantee of safety and relief from legal proceedings for himself and his supporters, and a firm assurance that the dethroned regime would not be allowed to return to office. Gen. Ironsi, like Nzeogwu, was an Ibo (or Igbo) man. The only known Igbo soldier killed by the Nzeogwu team was Col. Arthur Unegbe who was innocently discharging his duties as a soldier.

In a counter-coup that was initiated by the Northerners (Hausas) and a handful of Westerners (Yorubas) on July 29, 1966, ostensibly due to the assassination of some Northern and Western politicians by the Eastern (Ibo) dominated mutineers, notably (among the murdered politicians) Sir Abubakar Tafawa Balewa who was the Prime Minister, Chief Festus Okotie-Eboh, the Federal Finance Minister, Alhaji Ahmadu Bello, Premier of the defunct Northern Region, Chief Samuel L. Akintola, Premier of the defunct Western Region, among others, (they) seized the General and the Military Governor of the Western Region, Lt. Col. Adekunle Fajuyi, who was his host at Ibadan. Col. Fajuyi was appointed the Military Governor by the Ironsi administration.

General Aguiyi-Ironsi had gone to

Ibadan to hold a conference of twenty-four natural rulers from most parts of Nigeria after visiting the Northern Region. The address to the conference was almost the last official act by him before he was seized the following night. He made the mistake, according to some people, of not only believing on his crocodile symbol, but of having more of the unforgiving Hausas as his body-guards instead of people from his own tribe. He was later executed nearby with Lt. Col. Fajuyi, as a revenge against the fallen Hausa and a few Yoruba politicians. The irony was that Gen. Ironsi was not part, nor was he aware of the pending coup that brought him to power.

Lt. Col. (later Lt. Gen.) Theophilus Danjuma spear-headed the mutiny against Ironsi. He outwitted the Yorubas by sparing Ironsi's life in the North where he just visited, only to get him assassinated in the Yoruba land. Ever since then, the Ibos have remained suspicious of Yorubas to much greater degree. The report of their assassination came from Cotonou, Dahomey (now Benin Republic), but this was not officially confirmed in Nigeria until January 14, 1967 at the insistence of Lt. Col. Chukwuemeka Odumegwu Ojukwu. Lt. Col. Yakubu Gowon, the Army Chief of Staff, who on August 1, 1966 announced that he had taken over control of Nigeria after Brigadier Ogundipe, apparently shocked of the happenstance, refused to assume command, obviously knew that Gen. Ironsi and Lt. Col. Adekunle Fajuyi had been cruelly murdered shortly after their arrest. Gowon later promoted himself to General.

This counter-coup, in part, led to the outbreak of the Nigerian civil war. The then Eastern Region, under the governorship of Col. Chukwuemeka Odumegwu Ojukwu, declared independence as the Republic of Biafra on May 30, 1967, after warning that "the brutal and planned annihilation of officers of Eastern Nigeria origin" in the North and West, had cast a serious doubt as to whether the people of Nigeria could ever hope to live together honestly and sincerely as one nation.

Although Col. Ojukwu had viewed Col. Gowon as unfit for the enormous task ahead, the pogrom of the enterprising Ibos in the North and West in particular inevitably urged for the secession. Thus, a civil war ensued at the expense of the Nigerian unity and co-existence. Even though Gowon boasted that Nigeria would wipe out Biafra in 24 hours, the war lasted from 1967 to January 1970. At a stage, the Biafrans were a few miles away from capturing Lagos, the Nigerian capital, only to suffer a setback by saboteurs that was never reversed.

Although the Biafrans were almost starved to surrender because of the incessant blockade by the Nigerian armed forces with the help of the Cameroun Government under Ahidjo, on food and arms coming into the land-locked Biafra, the war ended with a declaration or communique of no victor, no vanquished by the two parties. "On Aburi we stand" popular slogan among Biafrans, gradually gave way for new but painful reconciliation era.

Major-General Philip Effiong, Biafran Chief of Staff who had been left in charge of Biafra as Gen. Ojukwu left for self exile, ordered his troops on January 12, 1970 to cease fighting. At a ceremony in Lagos on January 15, he formally proclaimed the end of the secession and accepted the authority of the Federal Government of Nigeria. On January 23, 1970, the government of Cote d'Ivoire (Ivory Coast) announced that it had granted Gen. Ojukwu a political asylum.

Again, in Nigeria, Gen. Yakubu Gowon was ousted on July 29, 1975 -- exactly nine years after Gen. Aguiyi-Ironsi was dethroned -- as he was attending an Organization of African Unity (OAU) meeting in Kampala, Uganda, by Brigadier (later General) Murtala Ramat Muhammed. It was a bloodless coup, and Gowon was retired with all military privileges. According to Gowon, he was aware of the coup before he left July 27, 1975 for the OAU meeting. One of his guards -- a captain -- had informed him of the imminent coup, but he did not want "heads to roll." From an objective point of view, it was a mere change of guards among Northerners.

On Friday, February 13, 1976, General Muhammed, who became popular because of his born-again stand on official corruption, dereliction of duty in Nigeria, and "standing tall" of a blackman in Africa, in an abortive coup, was assassinated by Lt. Col. Bukar Dimka. Muhammed, due to the mood of the nation, died a martyr, even to the Ibos whom he meted atrocities during the civil war. His treachery to Nigeria during the war was that he lost more troops than any commander in Nigerian history. Even Olusegun Obasanjo, his former colleague, in his book titled, My Command, described him as an undisciplined soldier.

This sudden exit of a charismatic leader created a vacuum that brought Brigadier (later General) Olusegun Obasanjo into the helm of affairs. Gen. Obasanjo became the first Yoruba man ever to head Nigeria, even though some detractors alleged that his acts were dictated by the Hausas that flanked him and dominated the Supreme Military Council. It was during his tenure, March 31, 1977, that President Jimmy (James) Carter arrived in Nigeria in the first official visit by an American President to Black Africa. President Carter officially took office on January 20, 1977. Andrew Jackson Young, an African American, was his U. N. Ambassador.

Gowon, unfortunately, by implication, was linked to the assassination of Gen. Muhammed where, thereafter, he became Head-of-State-turned-student in England. Any sympathy for Gen. Gowon who was considered a moderate by Nigerian standard, on how he handled the end of the civil war, was lost. The untoppled government stripped Gowon of all his military titles and entitlements. Britain rejected all diplomatic requests to extradite him.

Gen. Obasanjo handed power to the duly elected civilian government on October 1, 1979. Alhaji Shehu Usman Aliyu Shagari and Dr. Alexander Ifeanyichukwu Ekwueme took the mandates of president and vice-president respectively.

On December 31, 1983, the military boys showed up again. Gen. Muhammadu Buhari and his henchmen toppled the civilian government because of conspicuous corruption, faltering economy and ineptitude.

Said William F. Gutteridge in his book, The Military In African Politics, "The leaders of . . . coup were no exceptions to the rule that military leaders intervening in politics rarely have preconceived policies which they intend to apply. Essentially such groups begin by administering rather than governing: They are caretakers whose initial intention is often to end a trend of which they do not approve and to provide the framework within which government can be enabled to set off on a fresh course. They are not likely to have plans for wide-spread social change and the effect of their seizure of power may be virtually to wipe the political and constitutional slates clean."

This effectively describes the military intervention in Nigeria and Africa alike, up to this day.

Nonetheless, the revolution of Gen. Buhari and his Lieutenant, Brigadier (later Major-Gen.) Tunde Idiagbo did not last long. They were equally overthrown on August 27, 1985 by Gen. Ibrahim Badamosi Babangida who was Army Chief of Staff of Buhari administration. Babangida alleged that Buhari administration was infringing on the citizens rights by curbing their freedom of speech and civil liberties. He also alleged that they were more dictatorial than necessary.

His first official act was to repeal the treacherous and very unpopular decree No. 4 that banned free speech or attack to the government. Among other activities he later undertook was to reorganize the Nigerian Security Organization (NSO) and renamed it State Security Service (SSS). Later in his administration, he restored Yakubu Gowon's title back to general with all the rights and privileges appertaining to his forced retirement of July 29, 1975.

It must be mentioned that both Gowon and Ojukwu, the civil war Heads of State of Nigeria and Biafra respectively, who were generals during their tenure, were by irony of fate on self-exile on different reasons at different times, and were given presidential pardon by the civilian administration of Shehu Shagari within the same year. At the time of the pardon, neither Gowon nor Ojukwu's military title was restored. But Babangida, by a stroke of pen, simply restored that of Gowon. That, of course, irked Gen. Obasanjo (now retired) who stripped the title in the first place.

Babangida, the first military Head of State in Nigeria and probably in West Africa to claim the title of president without being elected, pledged to hand over power to the civilian government in 1990, but changed it to 1992. Barring any unforeseen circumstances, state legislators and governors would take their seats by 1990; presidential election would be in 1992. In 1987, Babangida "created" two more states in Nigeria, thus raising the number of states from 19 to 21. The names of the states are: Imo, Anambra, River, Cross River, Akwa Ibom (new), Bendel, Lagos (also capital), Oyo, Ogun, Ondo, Kwara, Benue, Plateau, Sokoto, Borno, Kaduna, Katsina (new), Kano, Gongola, Bauchi, and Niger. Effective from 1990, Abuja will be the new capital, other things being equal.

Babangida aborted a coup to his administration in December 1985 shortly after he took power. Some heads rolled. And the history of a relatively unstable Nigeria and the rancour, prevarication, and overzealousness of some of her citizens continue.

Ghana, capital Accra, was equally unstable. After the overthrow of Dr. Kwame Nkrumah, the no nonsense nationalist who led Ghana to independence on midnight, March 5-6, 1957, by Major-General Joseph A. Ankrah, formerly chief of Defence Staff of the Army and Col. Emmanuel Kwashie Kotoka, on February 24, 1966 while Dr. Nkrumah was on official visit to China, things have never been the same in Ghana. Since then, there have been coups and counter-coups.

While Ghana was ruled by the National Liberation Council formed by the coup leaders, President Sekou Toure of Guinea, on March 2, 1966, announced that Dr. Nkrumah had been appointed Joint Head of State of Guinea and Secretary-General of Guinea's sole political party. The ex-president's continued appeal over Radio Conakry to the people of Ghana on March 24, April 10 and 24, 1966 to overthrow the new regime failed to work.

In March 1968, Gen. Ankrah surrendered his responsibilities as Commander-in-Chief of the Armed Forces to Gen. A. Otu, who in turn was arrested on November 20, 1968 on suspicion of complicity in subversive activities. On September 30, 1969, it was officially announced that General Otu had been reinstated in the Armed Forces and that the Government having accepted the conclusions of a commission of inquiry had absolved the general of complicity. Gen. Otu was reappointed as Commander-in-Chief early in November 1969. Gen. Joseph A. Ankrah resigned as Head of State and chairman of the National Liberation Council on April 2, 1969, and was succeeded by Brigadier Akwasi Amankwa Afrifa. Gen. Ankrah's resignation stemmed from investigation into allegations that "certain persons had been collecting money from various companies, particularly expatriate firms, for building up political funds," and it was established that Gen. Ankrah was involved in the deal. He decided to resign hono(u)rably. However, Brigadier Afrifa, on April 8, 1969 promulgated a decree that would make such participation a serious offence.

In the general election to return to

civilian rule held August 29, 1969, and in some quarters regarded as the first free election since the pre-independence election in 1956, the Progress Party led by Dr. Kofia Busia who was in exile during Nkrumah's regime, won an unexpected overwhelming victory. He was sworn in as Premier on September 3, 1969 and members of the civilian cabinet announced on September 7. On October 1, 1969, he took full charge as Prime Minister.

On September 30, 1970, the National Assembly, upon a motion by Dr. Busia, supported by the opposition party, the presidential commission was unanimously dissolved. The chairman, Brigadier Akwasi Afrifa who was too young to qualify as a candidate for the office of the president, retired from the Army on August 7, 1970 after being promoted "In recognition of his service to Ghana."

Mr. Edward Akufo-Addo, a former Chief Justice fired by Dr. Nkrumah, and nominated by the Progress Party, was elected president of Ghana for a four-year term on August 28, 1970 in a secret ballot by the National Assembly. He defeated Dr. Isaac Asafu-Adjaye, a former member of the council of state.

On January 13, 1972, because of economic downturn and suppression of the opposition, Busia's regime was overthrown by Lt. Col. (later General) Ignatius Kutu

Acheampong, the acting commander of an Army Brigade.

On July 5, 1978, Acheampong, was quietly replaced as the Head of the Supreme Military Council by Lt. Gen. (later Gen.) Frederick Akuffo, the Chief of the Defence Staff.

On May 15, 1979, there was an unsuccessful coup attempt by Flight-Lt. John Jerry Rawlings. He was jailed for the coup attempt. However, on June 4, 1979, Rawlings was freed by his fellow junior officers and successfully executed a coup d' etat. In what he dubbed "House-cleaning", on June 16, 1979, Gen. Acheampong and Major-Gen. Utuka were executed by military firing squad. On June 26, Gen. Frederick Akuffo was shot, together with the highly regarded Lt. Gen. Akwasi A. Afrifa, Major-General Robert Kotei, Air Vice-Marshal George Boakye, Rear-Admiral Joy Amedume and Col. Roger Felli. A probe into corruption netted the government a sizeable seizure and some execution of those (found) guilty of crime of high magnitude.

As the "house cleaning" continued, national elections were held on June 18, 1979. The Peoples National Party led by Dr. Hilla Limann and Imoru Egala won a comfortable victory, securing overall majority. Dr. Limann, a medical practitioner from Tumu in the Upper Region was on September 24, 1979 sworn in as president and head of the government. This temporarily halted the military coups and reactionaryism.

On December 31, 1981, however, Rawlings seized power again, citing corruption and continuing economic malaise as the reasons for his action. He assumed chairmanship of Provisional National Defence Council. As of this writing, over eight years since he took back the power, he is yet to revive the economy of Ghana to an acceptable standard irrespective of all his good efforts. This time around, he knows for sure that uneasy lies the head that wears a crown, especially when one takes it by force as he did.

Egypt: From independence on February 28, 1922 till 1953, Egypt, with capital in Cairo, had been a monarchy state. Sultan Ahmed Fuad was proclaimed King of Egypt after independence from Britain. Egyptian Royal house had been founded by Mehemet Ali who was appointed Pasha of Egypt by the Sultan of Turkey in 1805, Egypt then forming part of the Ottoman Empire. The position of Pasha became hereditary among his descendants, who held the title of Khedive from 1867 and Sultan from 1914.

On July 23, 1952, General Mohammed Neguib, citing corruption and instability in the country, staged a successful bloodless military coup. This was the first military coup in Africa. The Premier, Hilaly Pasha "resigned" and was replaced by Aly Maher Pasha who formed a new government on July 24, 1952. On July 26, King Farouk was forced to abdicate his crown in favour of his infant son, the seven-month old Prince Ahmed Fuad. He left Egypt the same day. A Regency Council was appointed to hold the royal prerogatives until the infant came of age. When the government could not get itself rid of corruption, Gen. Neguib struck again. He took over the government and became the Prime Minister. Of course, Aly Maher was forced to resign. Lt. Col. Gamal Abdel Nasser was appointed Vice-Premier and minister of the interior.

Egypt became a republic on June 18, 1953 and Gen. Neguib assumed presidential powers as well as the role of the Prime Minister.

After Neguib, Col. Nasser became President. In a proclamation signed by President Nasser and President Kuwatly of Syria on February 1, 1958, the two republics of Egypt and Syria were merged into a single country -- The United Arab Republic.

However, on September 28, 1961, there was a successful military coup in Damascus to restore Syria's independence. Nonetheless, Egypt continued, unilaterally, to retain the name "United

Arab Republic."

On September 28, 1970, President Nasser died of a heart attack in Cairo. Anwar Sadat, Vice President of the country since December 20, 1969, was unanimously nominated for the presidency on October 5, 1970, by the eight-member Supreme Executive Committee of the Arab Socialist Union -- the only political party. On the national referendum (a mere rubber stamping) on October 15, 1970, Sadat received about 90.4 per cent of the total votes cast.

Following their military losses to Israel's soldiering might, Egypt was forced to enter into peaceful resolution to their differences. Initiated by President James (Jimmy) Earl Carter of the United States of America, Sadat succumbed into accepting Israel's right to exist. He paid a visit to Jerusalem with a reciprocating visit by Israeli Prime Minister Menachem Begin to Cairo in November, 1977 and December, 1977, respectively. A peace agreement dubbed Camp David Accords, named after Camp David where President Carter used to relax off the stress of weekdays work, was signed by Sadat and Israeli leader Menachem Begin in Washington, D.C. in March, 1979. Egypt paid the price of the peace accord by being ostracized by other Arab world.

On October 6, 1981, Sadat was

assassinated by the Moslem extremists as he was reviewing a parade celebrating Egypt's victory in the October 6, 1973 war with Israel. The assassins believed that he was being soft on Israel. Husni Mubarak, his right hand man, replaced him, with Fuad Muhiaddin as Prime Minister.

Sudan: Even Sudan, capital Khartoum, is not devoid of coups. On November 17, 1958, two years and ten months after its independence, the Sudanese Army, under the command of General Ibrahim Abboud, overthrew Abdullah Khalil government in a bloodless coup. He dissolved the parliament, banned all political activities and parties, and suspended the constitution.

In October 1964, the military regime was overthrown due to a popular uprising and revolt at Khartoum University in which one student was killed and eight others wounded by police on gun fire. An election was held for Constituent Assembly while Gen. Abboud would remain as President and Commander-in-Chief. In the new constitution, two thirds majority vote of the Assembly would override the President's veto. Nonetheless, on November 15, 1964, President Abboud resigned in accordance with "the people's desire to liquidate the military regime in all its forms" in politics. What a wish!

This wish notwithstanding, on May 25, 1969, Colonel Jaafar Mohammed al Nemery, in a bloodless coup d'etat, took over the government. Col. al Nemery later promoted himself to General and much later to Field Marshal.

Nemery's government happened to be the longest surviving regime in Sudan because he adopted the tactics of forming a predominantly civilian revolutionary council (cabinet). He named Sayyid Babiker Awadalla, a former Chief Justice, as Prime Minister. He was later replaced by Nemery who had been president of the revolutionary council and was subsequently elected the first President of Sudan. Under Nemery's leadership, the country was renamed Democratic Republic of Sudan.

Gen. Nemery personally participated in the resolution of the Jordanian crisis. In November 1970, it was declared that President Nemery, Kadhafi, and Sadat had decided to unite the Sudan, Libya and UAR (now Egypt) into one Federal state. This did not suit the communists who thereafter staged almost a successful coup which was led by Major Hashim al Ata on July 19, 1971. This led to a temporary overthrow of Gen. Nemery's regime, and the subsequent execution of some 30 officers who supported Nemery's policy. The communists' coup later proved abortive, because its proclaimed Head of State, Col. Babiker al Nur, and his aide, Major Faruq Hamadalla who were returning from London were forced down in Libya. The Libyan authorities handed them over to Nemery who had by chance regained control. This led to a massive purge of the communists. About 14 people were executed, including Major Hashim al Ata, Col Babiker al Nur, Major Faruq Hamadalla, and Joseph Garang who had been the Minister for Southern Affairs. The temporary regime controlled power for three good days.

Nonetheless, President Nemery was overthrown in a bloodless coup on April 6, 1985 as he was on official visit to the United States of America. There had been public discontent with his regime, exacerbated by substantial food and fuel price increases. Professionals in the country paralyzed the poor nation with strikes and civil disobedience. The inevitable coup was led by Lt. Gen. Swar al Dahab, recently appointed as the Minister of Defence and Commander-in-Chief of the Army by Nemery. As the news of the coup spread, like other trouble ridden developing countries, about one million people took to the streets in Khartoum, the capital, to celebrate.

Following the coup was the formation of a 15-member cabinet with Dr. Gizuli Dafallah, a trade unionist who spearheaded the general strike, as the Prime Minister. In the Transitional Military Council (TMC), a non-muslim southerner was also included.

In April 1986, a general election was held as promised by TMC. On May 15, 1986, a broadly based government was announced. The Council of Ministers consisted a coalition of Umma Party (UP) and Democratic Unionist Party (DUP) with Sadiq al Mahdi as the Prime Minister and Minister of Defence.

The TMC was dissolved as promised. On May 6, a six-member Supreme Council was inaugurated. Swar al Dahab was replaced by Gen. Tajeddin Abdullah Fadul, the vice-chairman of TMC as the Head of State and Commander-in-Chief of the Armed Forces.

Sudan is now ravaged by a religious ideological war between its Moslem North and the Christian South. The only solution to peace and tranquility to that poor nation seems to be the acceptance of secularism which the moslems are not keen to accept.

Central African Republic, with capital at Bangui, formerly known as Ubangui-Shari, had its independence on August 13, 1960. After its first Prime Minister, Barthelemy Boganda, died in an air crash in March 1959, David Dacko became his successor. Col. Jean-Bedel Bokassa, a cousin of Dacko, was made the Chief of Staff. On November 17, 1960, the National Assembly elected Dacko

President. In November 1962, however, the country became a one-party state.

On January 1, 1966, Bokassa staged a coup d'etat to preempt the promotion to power of Jean Izamo, head of the gendarmerie. Dacko was kept under house arrest. He, like Dacko, declared himself the spiritual descendant of Barthelemy Boganda, the "father of the nation." His despotism was virtually absolute. In 1972, he made himself president-for-life.

On September 20, 1979, as Bokassa was away in Libya seeking financial aid from Col. Gadhafi, he was deposed in a bloodless coup by his personal advisor, the former President David Dacko he dethroned. France, reportedly, helped in the coup.

Bokassa irked and alienated most people when in 1972 he made himself president-for-life; in 1974, he promoted himself to the rank of Marshal of the Republic, and in December 1976, he declared the end of the republic and then the formation of the Central African Empire.

When David Dacko took over after the coup, he restored the country to a republic. The French government managed to persuade President Felix Houphouet-Boigny of Ivory Coast to grant Bokassa a "humanitarian asylum."

On September 1, 1981, there was another coup. It succeeded. Gen. Andre Kolingba, formerly Chief of Staff, ousted Dacko and became the Head of State.

Benin Republic, formerly Dahomey, capital Porto Novo, with Hubert Maga as its first president as of December 31, 1960, after he served as Prime Minister since May 22, 1959, equally experienced coups d'etat. The country achieved its independence on August 1, 1960.

Following students and workers riots in October 1963, Col. Christophe Soglo, Commander of the Army, on October 28, 1963, deposed President Maga and formed a provisional regime which he would serve as the interim Head of State till January 1964 election. On November 27, 1963, Col. Soglo announced the discovery of a plot to kill him. He thereafter returned power to Ex-President Maga, who on December 3, 1963, resigned all his ministerial posts and was placed in detention.

On January 19, 1965, Sourou-Migan Apithy was elected President and Mr. Justine Ahomadegbe Vice-President.

On November 29, 1965, Apithy and Ahomadegbe resigned under pressure from the Army led by Gen. Soglo. Later Ahomadegbe was appointed in place of Apithy as President after Apithy refused to sign government decrees appointing the members of the Supreme Court, on the ground of unconstitutionality, and also declined to give his assent to a bill passed by the parliament, which laid down that the president of the Supreme Court could not be a politician.

Gen. Soglo, however, assumed supreme power on December 22, 1965, and dissolved the National Assembly and nullified the constitution.

Nonetheless, Gen. Soglo's regime was overthrown in a bloodless coup by the Army, led by Major Maurice Kouandete on December 17, 1967. Lt. Col. Alphonse Alley was named a Head of State with Major Maurice Kouandete as Prime Minister on December 21, 1967.

On June 28, Dr. Emile Derlin Zinsou was invested as president and entrusted with the formation of a government. During his installation as president on July 17, 1968, Dr. Zinsou announced that his appointment would be put to a referendum on July 28. This produced a firm vote of confidence for Dr. Zinsou.

On December 10, 1969, Dr. Zinsou's government was overthrown by the Army officers. A directorate consisting of Lt. Col. Emile de Souza, Lt. Col. Benoit Sinzogan, and Lt. Col. Maurice Kouandete was formed on December 12, 1969. Ex-Presidents Maga, Ahomadegbe and Apithy stated their support for Col. Kouandete and returned from exile shortly afterwards. The military ruled till the elections which took place in stages between March 3 - 31, 1970. All the four ex-presidents ran, almost all representing their regions. The election, however, was cancelled. The three rivals reached an agreement of ruling the government in turns for two-year periods each.

In October 1972, a coup led by Major (later Brig. General) Matthrew Kerekou, the Deputy Chief of Staff of the Armed Forces, took over power. He set up a 12-man National Revolutionary Council (NRC). Kerekou renamed Dahomey the "People's Republic of Benin" in December 1975 and launched a single party state known as parti de la revolution populair de Benin (PRPB).

Burundi, with capital at Bujumbura, formerly a Belgian-administered United Nations Trust Territory of Ruanda-Urundi, achieved independence as two separate states on July 1, 1962. The Southern part, Urundi, became the Kingdom of Burundi under the rule of Mwami (king) Mwambutsa IV, and the Northern part, Ruanda, became the Republic of Rwanda.

The establishment of the two states followed the failure of attempts engineered by the U.N. to bring about an agreement for the creation of a single independent nation comprising both halves of the territory. Both Ruanda and Urundi were once part of German East Africa before 1918, and were thereafter administered by Belgium as a League of Nations mandate.

However, the son of Mwami Mwambutsa, Prince Charles Ndizeye, on July 8, 1966, in a bloodless coup, overthrew his father and assumed the position of Head-of-State. He suspended the constitution and took the title of Ntari V. He appointed Capt. (later Lt. Gen.) Michel Micombero the Prime Minister on July 11, 1966. On September 1, 1966, the prince was crowned Mwami Ntari V.

On November 29, 1966, Micombero deposed Mwami Ntari and declared himself President and Burundi a Republic. With the abolition of the Monarchy, the most important stabilizing element in the political system of Burundi disappeared.

After dissolving the existing government, Micombero appointed a "Provisional Revolutionary Committee." The Uprona Party Central Executive, on December 2, 1966, approved all proposals to establish a presidential regime and a one-party state. On October 8, 1969, the president announced a failed coup attempt to overthrow his government in September. The alleged plotters were subsequently tried and executed.

Following a presidential election of

November, 1974, Micombero was re-installed as president of the republic. On November 1, 1976, Col. Jean-Baptiste Bagaza, a former Deputy Chief of Staff, staged a bloodless coup and overthrew the Micombero government. Micombero fled to Somalia where he died in July 1983.

Bagaza was a Tutsi-Hima (a "minority" tribe) from Rutovu in the south. He was, however, overthrown on September 4, 1987 by Pierre Buyoya who vowed to end the ethnic differences between Hutu, the "majority," and Hutsi, the ruling minority. This wish did not materialize as about 40,000 Hutu people were killed, thousands wounded, and about 120,000 fled to neighbouring Rwanda in August 1988 in a tribal conflict with Hutsi people who controlled the government.

Cameroun: Ahmadou Ahidjo who became Prime Minister since February 1958 under a statute of 1956, whereby the territory received internal autonomy while remaining under French Trusteeship, became President of Cameroun, capital Yaounde, after independence on January 1, 1960.

In November 1982, after 22 years in power, President Ahidjo resigned, handing power to his Prime Minister, Paul Biya. Although no official reason was given, the abdication of power was as a result of a false medical report of "bribed"

Ahidjo doctors who advised him to resign from his hectic post to avoid worsening his "ailing" health.

The new President, Biya, a bilingual christian southerner, had been Ahidjo's right hand man. He appointed Bello Bouba Maigari, a northerner, as Prime Minister in a cabinet reshuffle. Ahidjo, however, retained the chairmanship of the UNC party.

Nonetheless, Biya decided to break the link with Ahidjo by reshuffling his cabinet to his own liking. Because of this, there was an unsuccessful military coup that rocked the very foundation of the country. Due to his implication and that of the Northern soldiers in the abortive coup d'etat, Ahidjo fled to Southern France in a voluntary exile and later to Senegal. He was sentenced to death in absentia. In 1988, Biya was reelected under the banner of his country's one-party system.

Chad: As a small country as Chad, with capital at N'Djamena is, it has probably seen more troubles and instability than any independent African nation. Its first President at independence was Francois (later Ngarta) Tombalbaye. In August 1973, he urged all christians (he was a protestant) to change their names to native ones. He changed his from Francois to Ngarta. The capital of the country, originally known as Fort-Lamy became N'Djamena and streets with "foreign" names were also changed. Muslims, however, preserved their first names even if they were of Arab origin. This was part of his instrument of national renewal and "authenticity."

On April 13, 1975, Tombalbaye was assassinated during a military coup organized by young officers and the gendarmerie, joined at the last moment by the interim Chief of Staff, Gen. Mbailau Odingar. The President was accused of having "despised the Armed Forces, cast a slur on national unity and of pursuing disastrous economic policies." Gen. Felix Malloum, detained since 1973, was released on April 15, 1975 and made President of a supreme military council comprised of nine officers.

The new government quickly had an opposition led by Hissene Habre of the Front de Liberation National du Tchad (FROLINAT) formed in 1960 in Sudan. Habre was later replaced by Goukouni Oueddei, the son of a Derde, a customary chief among the Teda in the Tibesti. In fact, there was a sporadic war within the country. In the war, FROLINAT was defeated while a conference of unity was going on in Tripoli Libya in July 1978 between the leaders -- Malloum and Goukouni -- with the involvement of Libya, Sudan, and Niger Republic. After a series of talks, an agreement was reached between Malloum and Habre on

August 25, 1978. Four days later, a "charte fondamentale" was promulgated. Malloum remained the President while the former rebel leader, Habre, became Prime Minister.

Hostilities broke out within the FROLINAT and the appointment of Habre deepened the situation. Habre was establishing a position as the champion of Islamic North against the christian South. Cooperation between Habre and Malloum fell apart as Malloum refused to grant special privileges to the muslims. Hence, war started between Habre's troops and Forces armees tchadiennes (FAT), the legal state army under the supreme authority of President Malloum. Habre's troops outclassed the government forces.

In a Kano (Nigeria) conference of the warring parties and the representatives of Niger, Cameroun, Nigeria, Libya and Sudan, chaired by the Nigerian Army General, Shehu Yar'Adua on March 12 - 16, 1979, an agreement was reached. The four factions of Chad were FAT (Malloum), FAP (Goukouni), FAN (Habre) and the Mouvement Populaire pour la Liberation du Tchad (MPLT) or Troisieme armee, a splinter group from FAP having close links with Nigeria and led by Aboubakar Mahamet Abderamane.

On March 16, 1979, the Kano agreement was signed. It provided for a cease-fire, the demilitarization of

N'Djamena, the liberation of political prisoners and hostages, the dissolution of existing government bodies, the formation of a Gouvernement d'union nationale du transition (GUNT) and the creation of an integrated army. Nigeria was to send a neutral force to maintain security in N'Djamena.

On March 23, 1979, Malloum and Habre resigned, and a provisional state council of eight members (two from each faction) was constituted under the presidency of Goukouni Oueddei. Goukouni later became the President of Chad, although with some dissention, such as Habre who entered into war with him again.

On June 7, 1982, FAN forces of Habre gained ground and finally entered N'Djamena unopposed by the government forces. Goukouni fled to Cameroun and thence, to Algeria. Habre later consolidated his position and power. Despite all Libyan incursions, he stood his ground. Libya later had a change of heart. The two countries on Monday, October 3, 1988, restored full diplomatic relations between themselves up to the ambassadorial level; thus giving peace a chance.

Comoros: In Comoros, the Comoran Chamber of Deputies, on July 6, 1975, approved a unilateral declaration of independence. The next day, the chamber elected Ahmed Abdallah to be the

-158-

president of the new state. The chamber constituted itself as the National Assembly of the small island.

Abdallah immediately faced opposition from the Front National Union (FNU), a group of parties in favour of more conciliatory policy towards Mayotle -- an island that remained linked to France -- and opposed to Abdallah's personal power. On August 3, 1975, the FNU staged a coup in Moroni, and Abdallah was overthrown.

Following the dissolution of the National Assembly, a national executive council was formed, headed by Said Mohammed Jaffar, comprising representatives of all the islands, including Mayotle. Ali Soilih, the leader of the coup, became the Defence and Interior Minister. He was, however, elected Head of State on January 2, 1976 to replace Prince Said Mohammed.

In May 1978, Soilih was equally overthrown in an easy coup, carried out by about 50 European mercenaries led by a Frenchman, Major Bob Denard, on behalf of the exiled Ex-President Abdallah. Soilih was assassinated a fortnight later, allegedly while trying to escape from house arrest. The government was taken over by a "politico-military directory," with Abdallah and his former deputy, Muhammed Ahmed, as co-presidents.

As a result of the method of this coup, Comoros was expelled from the ministerial council of the Organization of African Unity. In February 1979 though, the Comoran delegation was readmitted to the OAU, a sign that the new regime had eventually been accepted. On October 1, 1978 referendum, a constitution creating a Federal Islamic Republic was approved. On October 22, 1978, Abdallah was elected President for a six-year term.

The People's Republic of Congo, (formerly Congo Brazzaville) achieved her independence on August 15, 1960 with Abbe Fulbert Youlou as the president. President Youlou was overthrown by the army on August 15, 1963 after meeting with Trade Union leaders who were to call for a strike on August 13, but were arrested on August 12, 1963. Mr. Youlou and his family escaped from detention on March 25 - 26, 1965. He was sentenced to death in absentia on June 8, 1965.

The Army helped to hold elections on December 8, 1963. Alphonse Massemba-Debat was elected unopposed as president on December 19, 1963 and Pascal Lissouba was appointed Prime Minister on December 24, 1963.

As a result of an unrest in which the Attorney-General, the Director of Government Information Agency, and the President of the Supreme Court were killed on February 15, 1965, allegedly by the gangs of Jeunesse members, President Massemba-Debat, on a pressure from the Army, withdrew from the capital on August 2, 1968. The Army assumed power on August 3, 1968 but failed to muster sufficient popular support. They recalled the President. A day after his return, the President announced the formation of a Counseil National de la Revolution (CNR) which would "coordinate the policies of the government and CNR and control and direct the action of the state." This would be led by the Chief of General Staff, Col. Marien Ngouabi.

On September 3, 1968, Massemba-Debat was dismissed. This was announced on September 4, 1968. The Army took over again. The provisional government was headed by Capt. Alfred Raoul who had been appointed Prime Minister on August 22, 1968. On September 5, Capt. Raoul also took over the functions of Head of State and Defence.

On January 1, 1969, the CNR nominated Col. Marien Ngouabi, the Army Commander, as Head of State with Major Raoul as Prime Minister. It was Ngouabi who renamed the country The People's Republic of Congo.

After many attempts on his life, President Ngouabi was assassinated on March 18, 1977, in what was claimed to be an unsuccessful coup attempt by supporters of the former president, Massemba-Debat, a member of the rival tribe. In the military tribunal that ensued for the trial of the chief figures connected with the coup, on March 25, 1977, Massemba-Debat was executed.

Due to uncertainties in the country, martial law was swiftly imposed by the military Committee of the Parti Congolais du Travail (PCT) originally formed in December 1969 by Ngouabi -- a Marxist-Leninist vanguard party. Col. (later Brig. General) Joachim Yhombi-Opango was nominated as the new Head of State.

Because of his dictatorial attitude, Yhombi-Opango was dumped during the congress of PCT. When the congress meeting was held at the end of March 1979, Col. Denis Sassou-Nguesso, a follower of Ngouabi, a long time rival of Yhombi-Opango, was appointed Head of State, President and Chairman of the Central Committee. A new Council under Major (later Col.) Louis Sylvain Goma, the Prime Minister was announced on April 4, 1979.

Equatorial Guinea had its independence on October 12, 1968, with Senor Francisco Macias Nguema as her first President. Fernando Poo was one of her famous island provinces. President Nguema later became authoritarian. In July 1972, he declared himself President-for-life. He exercised absolute power.

On August 3, 1979, a successful coup was staged by Lt. Col. Teodoro Obiang Nguema Mbasogo, the Commander of the National Guard and a nephew of the President. On September 29, 1979, President Senor Macias Nguema was executed. Mbasogo, who is now a general, remains in power. He was recently accused by Nigeria of having an economic cooperation with the racist South Africa.

<u>Guinea</u>, with capital at Conakry, gained her independence on October 2, 1958. Its first President until his death on March 26, 1984 was Sekou Toure. Since 1947, he had been Secretary-General of the Parti democratique de Guinea (PDG) which was constitutionally established on November 10, 1958 as the country's only political party.

After suffering a heart attack, he was flown from Guinea to the U.S.A., where he died during emergency surgery on March 26, 1984.

Before the now leaderless government group could choose a successor who would exert control, the Army staged a coup d'etat on April 3, 1984. They formed Comite militaire de redressement national (CMRN). This was largely comprised of middle and lower ranking army officers. The principal leaders were Cols. Lansana Conte and Diara Traore, who became President and Prime Minister respectively. In a government reshuffle in December 1984, the post of Prime Minister was abolished. Conte's close associate, Col. Traore, was demoted to Minister of State for national education.

On July 4, 1985, while Conte was on Economic Community of West African States (ECOWAS) summit meeting in Togo, Col. Traore attempted a coup d'etat that failed. The loyal army to Conte regained control. Traore and Ex-President Sekou Toure's half-brother, Ismael Toure, were later executed. Conte promoted himself to the rank of Brigadier General.

<u>Guinea Bissau</u>, under the leadership of Luiz Cabral, the brother of the assassinated founder of Partido Africano de Independencia da Guinee Cabo verde, Amilcar Cabral, gained her independence on September 10, 1974.

On November 14, 1980, the Prime Minister, Joao Vieira, led a coup in which the Cabral regime was overthrown, and Cabral himself placed under house arrest. This was quickly followed by the abolition of the National Assembly and the State Council. They were replaced by a new Revolutionary Council of nine members, of which six of them were soldiers.

<u>Lesotho</u> gained her independence on October 4, 1966 with Prince Seeiso as King Moshoeshoe II, and Chief Leabua

Jonathan the Prime Minister.

Chief Jonathan's lean towards Communist bloc, his refusal to expel the African National Congress (ANC) activists from Lesotho, and his disdainful, though necessary attitude, in signing a joint security treaty with South Africa, prompted the Pretoria government, in early 1986, to effectively close the land frontiers between the two countries; thus, halting the flow of essential supplies into the kingdom.

On January 15, 1986, with the economy seriously crippled as a result of the blockade and a threat by Prime Minister Jonathan of seeking help from Soviet Union and Cuba if none was forthcoming from the United Kingdom and United States of America, troops of the Lesotho paramilitary forces, led by Maj. Gen. Justin Lekhanga surrounded the government buildings and the Youth League Headquarters. On January 20, 1986, Lekhanga who had recently returned from "security consultation" with the apartheid South Africa, together with Major Gen. S. K. Molapo, the commander of the security forces, and S. R. Matela, the chief of police, deposed the Jonathan government. They established a military council headed by Justin Lekhanga, including five other senior officers of the paramilitary force.

On January 27 and 28, 1986, a

council of ministers was sworn in, comprising three officers and 17 civilians, mostly civil servants and professional men, including a former member of Jonathan's cabinet. The National Assembly was dissolved, and all executive and legislative powers were vested on the King, acting on the advice of the military council.

Madagascar had her independence on June 26, 1960 with Philibert Tsiranana, a school teacher of the Tsimihety tribe who was also the leader of Parti Social Democrate (PSD) as the President.

On May 13, 1972, two weeks after his third inauguration as president, riots broke out in Tananarive between the security forces and a coalition of students, teachers, labourers, and urban unemployed citizens. After three days of violence in which 34 persons were killed, Tsiranana gave full powers to Gen. Gabriel Ramanantsoa, an apolitical Merina who was chief of staff of Madagascar's Armed Forces.

In a move that stunned military coup observers, on February 5, 1975, Ramanantsoa who just reshuffled his cabinet, handed his powers over to Col. Richard Ratsimandrava, who may well have organized this "legal coup." But six days later, he was assassinated in circumstances that had never been fully explained. Immediately after his elimination, an 18-man military directorate, which included Lt. Commander Didier Ratsiraka, was formed under Gen. Gilles Andriamahazo, who retained his predecessor's cabinet, while at the same time having his regime formally approved by the Higher Council on Institutions (CSI).

On June 15, 1975, Didier Ratsiraka was invested with the honour of Head of State and Head of the Government. He became popular as a renowned diplomat and intransigent nationalist, particularly as he was not tainted by any involvement with Col. Richard Ratsimandrava's brief government or assassination.

Mali, the former French Sudan, became independent on September 22, 1960 under the leadership of President Modibo Keita. It later became a one-party state, and Union Soudanaise party pursued socialist policies based on extensive nationalization of the economy.

On November 19, 1968, a group of young military officers staged a successful coup d'etat. A 14-member comite militaire pour la liberation nationale (CMLN) was set up with Lt. (later Gen.) Moussa Traore as President and Captain Yoro Diakite as head of the government. Ex-president Modibo Keita died in detention in May 1977. This brought out an unprecedented demonstration hostile to the ruling government.

In the presidential and legislative election held in June 1979 in which Modibo Keita's former political associates were barred, Traore retained the presidential position. In a major reshuffle in June 1986, he appointed Dr. Mamadou Dembele the new post of Prime Minister.

Algeria: Algeria, which was invaded in 1830 by the order of Charles X on his quest for expansionism, gained her independence on July 3, 1962. France granted this fiercely fought independence after about 250,000 Frenchmen and Algerians had given their lives in what was more or less a civil war. The capital of Algeria is Algiers.

In 1963, one of the rebel leaders, Ahmed Ben Bella, became Algeria's first President. He proclaimed Algeria a socialist state and urged the workers to take over and manage the businesses and farms abandoned by colons who fled the country out of fear and depredation.

In 1965, Houari Boumedienne, the Army Commander, overthrew the Ben Bella government. He began rapid economic development. His aggressive economic programme put Algeria atop many third world countries. That success in part justified his military intervention. He, however, died in 1978.

In 1979, Chadli Bendjedid, the Defence Minister, was elected President. He was reelected in 1984.

Mauritania: From the country's independence on November 28, 1960, until a military coup in 1978, Mauritania was ruled by Moktar Ould Daddah, who became Prime Minister in 1959 when his party, Parti du Regroupement Mauritanien (PRM) won all the seats in the general elections.

In July 1978, Ould Daddah was overthrown in a bloodless military coup. Full powers were assumed by a Military Committee for National Recovery (CMRN) under the chairmanship of the Chief of Staff, Lt. Col. Moustapha Ould Salek. In 1979, Ould Salek consolidated his powers. He replaced CMRN with Military Committee for National Salvation (CMSN) with 13 members.

In June 1979, Ould Salek resigned and was replaced by Lt. Col. Mohamed Louly who was the Minister of Public Works. In July 1979, Lt. Col. Mohamed Khouna Haidalla, the Prime Minister announced Mauritania's withdrawal from the Western Sahara, and renunciated any territorial claims on the Western Sahara, now Saharawi Arab Democratic Republic.

In January 1980, Lt. Col. Haidalla

displaced Louly as President and dismissed members of CMSN who were allegedly "impeding national recovery." He took neutral ground on the Western Sahara conflict. Opposition movement, however, developed, notably the Parti Islamique, established in Rabat by the former Air Force Commander, Lt. Col. Mohamed Abdelkader who lost his position in the Louly government in June 1979.

In December 1980, Haidalla formed a civilian government with Ahmed Ould Bneijara as Prime Minister. He permitted a multi-party system. On December 26, a number of arrests were carried out following the discovery of an alleged Libyan-inspired plot to take over the government and merge Mauritania, the Western Sahara and Libya into a single state. There were other foiled attempted coups in Haidalla's government. In April 1981, Haidallah dumped Ould Bneijara for his brief flirtation with Libya. He was replaced by Lt. Col. (later Col.) Maawiya Ould Sid' Ahmed Taya, the Chief of Staff.

As Haidalla left for a Franco-African summit meeting in Burundi, Col. Taya, in a quiet and bloodless coup d'etat, on December 12, 1984, deposed him. He accused Haidalla of wasteful spending and corruption. He returned home to face detention. In 1985, Col. Taya initiated a series of substantial and significant changes in both the economy, administration, and policies that attracted the support of the World Bank and major donor countries. In a reshuffle, he appointed three men that served under Ex-President Ould Daddah's government. He officially pardoned the ex-president and invited him to return home from exile. He equally released many political prisoners while maintaining his country's recognition of Polisario and Saharawi Arab Democratic Republic (SADR). Polisario Front was formed on May 20, 1973 to fight for Western Sahara independence.

Niger Republic, with capital at Niamey, had independence on August 3, 1960. Hamani Diori who was the Prime Minister was unanimously elected President of the Republic by the National Assembly on November 9, 1960.

Diori, like Felix Houphouet-Boigny of Cote d'Ivoire (Ivory Coast) aligned with France as well as Cote d'Ivoire. French management was maintained at the same level as before independence in both the administrative and commercial life of the country. A French military garrison was maintained in Niamey. Things went well for Diori, including success in suppressing opposition until the wicked drought of 1973 -- at its worst stage.

On April 15, 1974, the Army Chief of Staff, Lt. Col. Seyni Kountche, in a bloody coup that eliminated the wife of the President, took the helm of affairs.

The resistance he encountered was only at Diori's palace. The now ex-president and most of his ministers were imprisoned. Kountche set up Conseil militaire Supreme (CMS) to rule on the principle of effective action to distribute food aid and restore morality to public life.

About 100 political prisoners were released and the military showed a desire for reconciliation in the country. Djibo Bakary, the leader of opposition Sawaba party banned from the country, returned from exile. About 200 men of French military contingent were expelled. None of these tarnished Niger's relationship with France.

On October 6, 1983, as President Kountche was out of the country, there was an unsuccessful coup by officers close to him. He, however, died in November 1987 in Paris while receiving medical treatment for his ailment. He died of natural causes. He was eulogized in Africa for his contribution to his country.

After the death of Kountche, Ali Saibou, also a military officer, took over the rein of authority. He plans a one-party state for his country. He claimed that "one-party system is not incompatible with pluralism in the expression of opinions." No doubt, he wants to be the sole candidate.

Rwanda gained her independence on July 1, 1962 with Gregoire Kayibanda as the President, a year after the abolition of monarchy in September 1961 through a referendum. Although a serious tribal strife between the majority Hutu tribe and Tutsi broke out in December 1963, Kayibanda was reelected in 1969.

Due to the rift between the Northerners, Central and Southern region politicians, the Defence Minister and Head of the National Guard, Major General Juvenal Habyarimana, a Northerner from Gisenyi, on July 5, 1973, overthrew the government in a bloodless coup. He proclaimed a second republic and established a military administration with the banner of Committee for National Peace and Unity. This was used as the instrument for governing until August, when a new Council of Ministers, with Major Gen. Habyarimana as president was constituted.

In 1976, Rwanda, Burundi, and Zaire established the Economic Community of the Great Lakes Countries. In July 1975, during the second anniversary of the second Republic, President Habyarimana announced the formation of a new party-- Mouvement Revolutionaire National pour le Development (MRND) -- intended to include representatives of the military and civilian sectors.

The principal objective of the new

party was to eradicate regional and ethnic hatreds, while at the same time, promoting rural development. The Army Chief, who was the sole candidate, was, however, reelected president in 1979.

Seychelles gained her independence on June 29, 1976 with James Mancham as President of the new Republic and Albert Rene, as Prime Minister. Aldabra, Desroches, and Farquhar islands were returned to Seychelles. They had been detached from the archipelago in 1965 to form part of the British Indian Ocean Territory and placed for 50 years at the U.S.A.'s disposal for military purposes.

The coalition government was expected to remain in office until the 1979 elections, but on the night of June 4-5, 1977, supporters of the socialist oriented Seychelles People's United Party (SPUP), led by the Prime Minister, Albert Rene, staged an armed coup d'etat as Mancham was in London for the Commonwealth conference. It was reported that some 60 Seychellois secretly received arms and training from Tanzania before the coup in which several people were killed. Although Rene denied any fore-knowledge of the coup, he was, nonetheless, sworn in as president. He formed a new government. Ever since then, there had been attempted coups with no success.

Libya, with capital at Tripoli,

officially became independent on December 24, 1951. It was formerly a possession of the Ottoman Empire but ceded to Italy by Turkey under the Treaty of Ouchy in October 1912.

The country was provisionally placed under British and French administrations after World War II -- the two territories of Cyrenaica and Tripolitania under British, and Fezzan under French. The official language of Libya is Arabic.

A resolution of the United Nations Assembly of November 21, 1949 laid down that Libya should become independent before January 1, 1952. On December 3, 1950, the Libyan Constituent Assembly adopted a resolution formally proclaiming Mohamed Sayed Idris el-Senussi, the Emir of Cyrenaica as King of Libya. It equally declared that Libya should be an independent and sovereign state. Libya became the United Kingdom of Libya.

On September 1, 1969, King Idris was toppled in a bloodless military coup carried out by a group of young officers. His apparent heir, crown Prince Hassan al Rida, announced his voluntary abdication and expressed his support for the new regime. A revolutionary council was formed to exercise all executive and legislative powers. Libya was renamed Libyan Arab Republic.

On September 8, a Republic

government comprising two army officers and seven civilians responsible to the Revolutionary Council was announced. This was headed by Dr. Mahmond Soliman al Maghrabi.

Apart from the identity of the chairman, Colonel Moamer al Kadhafi, the membership of the Revolutionary Council, now consisting of 12 officers, was not made public until January 10, 1970. A new constitution published on December 11, 1969, described Libya as a "free democratic Republic," and that the Revolutionary Council, "The highest authority in the Libyan Arab Republic," would have the prerogatives of appointing the council of ministers (cabinet), signing and modifying treaties, declaring wars, etc.

On January 16, 1970, a new cabinet was announced, headed by Col. Kadhafi who replaced Dr. Maghabi as premier. He then pushed and succeeded in the withdrawal of all British and U.S.A. military bases from Libya. On July 21, 1970, Col. Kadhafi announced that his government had decreed the confiscation of all assets in Libya owned by Italians. Italy's protest did not yield a change of heart.

Col. Kadhafi has remained in power since then. He was, however, shaken when the U.S. Air Force, by the order of President Ronald Reagan, bombed Libya in April 1986 in an effort to get rid of him. Kadhafi's 13-month old adopted child was killed during the bombardment. The U.S. allegedly lost about two aircrafts in the deadly mission, although the U.S. government claimed that it lost only one with two Air Force personnel on board. Both of them died.

Luckily for Kadhafi, who hardly slept at one place twice consecutively, he was not at the place the U.S.A. and Israeli intelligence agents thought that he was. He was at large for several days. He emerged later, but not as fierce as he used to be.

The U.S. official reason for their action, an apparent unconstitutional attempt to assassinate the Head of State of another nation, was that Libya, allegedly was sponsoring state terrorism. The U.S. war planes took off for the operation from their British air base after Margaret Thatcher, the British Prime Minister, who had a tendentious attitude toward Kadhafi and his Libya, okayed the diplomatic request for the attack. Toward the tail end of Ronald Reagan's final term (his term officially ended as Bush was sworn in on January 20, 1989), his administration cropped up another accusation that Libya had a chemical weapons plant. Reagan could not muster world condemnation of Libya as a licence for another bombing.

Burkina Faso, formerly Upper Volta,

became an independent republic on August 5, 1960. On December 8, Maurice Yameogo, who had been Prime Minister since October 1958 when the country was an autonomous Republic with the French Community, was unanimously elected President by the National Assembly.

On January 3, 1966, following a general strike and demonstration by trade union, President Yameogo's regime was deposed by the Army Chief of Staff, Lt. Col. (later General) Sangoule Lamizana. On January 5, 1966, he suspended the constitution and dissolved the National Assembly. He exercised legislative and executive powers by ordinance and decrees.

In an effort to fulfill the promise they made during their coup, the military, in 1970, planned a quasi-civilian rule. Gen. Lamizana would remain as the President while there would be election of the National Assembly and civilian Prime Minister. Finally, Gerard Ouedraogo became the Prime Minister and Joseph Ouedraogo (no relation to Gerard) became the National Assembly President.

In January 1974, the government grounded to a halt due to a stalemate between the Prime Minister and the National Assembly. The Assembly refused to pass any further legislation until Prime Minister Gerard Ouedraogo resigned. On February 8, 1974, however, President

Lamizana announced that the military had taken over the government. He dissolved the Assembly and suspended the constitution, except freedom of the press and trade union. Political activities were banned and a curfew was imposed. A new government of national renewal in which 10 out of 14 senior posts were military officers was formed. Gen. Lamizana once again ruled by decree.

By 1977, the citizens were fully poised for civilian government. This forced Lamizana to go that route. President Lamizana again ran in the ticket for the presidency. He was once more returned to power, this time for five years after a run-off election with Macaire Ouedraogo. He got 56% of the vote during the run-off election with Ouedraogo 43%.

Due to the incessant political rivalries, both in government and political parties, Col. Saye Zerbo, the military commander of the capital region, in November 1980, toppled President Lamizana's government in a bloodless military coup. He formed a Comite militaire de redressement pour le progres national (CMRPN) to take over the government. A curfew was imposed, the National Assembly dissolved, and the constitution once again suspended. The military was quick to add that all liberties except political ones would be guaranteed. In December 1980, a CMRPN decree made public a new council of ministers in which all key posts went to the military.

Nonetheless, on November 7, 1982, a group of non-commissioned officers ousted Zerbo's regime and issued a statement lambasting Zerbo for corruption, suppression of liberties and arrests of workers and students as the government did in April 1982.

A provisional council for the people's salvation was formed. It was made up of corporals, sergeants and officers up to the rank of major, with Surgeon-Major Jean-Baptiste Ouedraogo as chairman, Head of State and Minister of Defence. Col. Gabriel Some, Chief of Staff and some other ministers under Zerbo were retained.

Although it was rumoured that Capt. Thomas Sankara, who was removed from the Information Ministry by CMRPN was implicated in the coup, his formal inclusion in the new regime was not confirmed until January 1983, when he was appointed the Prime Minister.

By May 1983, it became obvious that there was a division within the army. A compromise in the army between the traditionalists led by the Chief of Staff, Col. Some, and the radicals led by Capt. Sankara began to fall apart. The last straw in early May 1983 was a visit by the Libyan leader, Col. Moamer Kadhafi to Upper Volta at Sankara's invitation. A few days after Kadhafi's departure, Jean-Baptiste Ouedraogo ordered the arrest of Sankara and his radical colleagues in the conseil de salut du peuple (CSP). Libyan charge d'affaires was expelled. Sankara was accused of "dangerously threatening national unity."

Shortly after Sankara's arrest, the members of his commando unit in Po, near the Ghanaian border, instantly rebelled against his arrest. Col. Some, who was then in charge of the national defence, was accused of masterminding the arrest. France, whose presidential adviser on African Affairs, Guy Penne, probably by coincidence, was in Ouagadougou, the capital, was accused of influencing the affair. The Po commandos, now led by Capt. Blaise Compaore, took control of the town and refused orders from the Capital. The group demanded the dismissal of Col. Some and the unconditional release of Sankara. Eventually, Capt. Sankara was released unconditionally, but Ouedraogo was unwilling to dismiss Some. The open confrontation later spread to other barracks.

On August 4, 1983, the regime of Ouedraogo was overthrown by Sankara in a military coup. In the attacks and counter-attacks between the opposing forces during the bloody coup, Col. Some was killed. In consolidating his powers, Capt. Sankara installed a conseil national de la revolution (CNR) and formed a new government with himself as Head of State and Capt. Blaise Compaore as Minister of State to the presidency.

The CNR which was composed of junior officers and non-commissioned officers proceeded to effect wide-ranging measures. It won the support of a left-wing civilian group previously underground as Lique Patriotique pour le developpement (LIPAD).

Having the Ghanaian leader, Flight-Lt. Jerry Rawlings as a reference order, Capt. Sankara established the comites pour la defense de la revolution (CDR) all across the country. A revolutionary "people's tribunal" was constituted to hold trials on the former public officials. In November 1983, a joint military exercise was held with Ghana. The new tribunal, accordingly, began work in January 1984.

The first to be tried, but acquitted for squandering official funds was the Ex-President Lamizana. In April, Ex-President Zerbo was imprisoned for 15 years, seven of them suspended but ordered to reimburse 61 million francs he had allegedly misappropriated from public funds. In June, Gerard Ouedraogo, the former UDU party leader, was sentenced to 10 years with six years suspended for embezzlement. The former Prime Minister, Joseph Conombo, was given a suspended sentence on similar charges.

On August 3, 1984, during the first anniversary of the coup that brought him to power, Capt. Thomas Sankara changed the name of his nation from its colonial given name of Upper Volta to Burkina Faso -- meaning in the local Mossi and Dioula languages, land of the upright men -- to symbolize the political cornerstone that was taking place. He instituted other amiable policies that benefitted not only his 7.3 million fellow citizens, but that stole the heart of Africa, especially his undisguised bitter policies against apartheid in South Africa.

But this was not to last too long to the amazement of Africans. He was assassinated by his closest friend and associate. Said the Time Magazine (of USA) of October 26, 1987, Capt. Sankara who was 37 years at the time of his death, was "a populist who religiously consulted with the village leaders before embarking on new policies . . . made personal probity a point of hono(u)r in a country that has had more than one corrupt leader since winning independence in 1960."

Sankara, who was a popular and charismatic leader, and by "every inch an upright man" according to Time Magazine, was actually eliminated. He was ousted and coldly murdered in a bloody rebellion led by his friend and second in command, Captain Blaise Compaore, 36, who was the Minister of State and Justice, on October 15, 1987. Capt. Sankara was hastily buried along with about a dozen others killed during the coup in a mass grave on the outskirts of Ouagadougou, the capital, while his family watched in tears and disbelief.

Capt. Sankara used to boast of being the lowest paid head of state in the world, with a salary of only $450.00 per month. In a radio announcement following the outrageous coup, he was accused of "concentration of power" and harbouring the "ambitions of a madman."

Nonetheless, to the credit and relief of the fallen hero, the national radio, following the pronouncement, quickly concurred that his policies' basic wisdom "is not called into question." This forces one to ask, why was he unceremoniously murdered and dethroned? Capt. Compaore has had a hard time trying to explain his reasons. No one was buying it, however.

The acute cruelty manifested in the assassination of Capt. Thomas Sankara, coupled with his unwholesome burial, catapulted him to martyrdom. And that dwarfs anything Capt. Blaise Compaore might do in the interest of his nation, assuming he has anything new to offer other than his fantasy of power.

Sierra Leone, with its capital at Freetown, was not spared of political crisis. It received its independence on April 27, 1961 within the commonwealth through the leadership of Dr. (later Sir) Milton Margai who had been the Prime Minister since 1958. When Sir Margai died in April 1964, his half-brother, Dr. (later Sir) Albert Margai, previously the Minister of Finance, succeeded him as Prime Minister.

During March 1967 general elections, the opposition party, All-People's Congress (APC), led by Siaka Stevens, won more seats in the House of Representatives than Sir Albert Margai's Sierra Leone People's Party (SLPP). As a result, Brig. David Lansana, head of the army and Margai's strong supporter, staged a coup d'etat on March 23, to prevent Stevens from assuming power, which he believed was being given to him illegally by the Governor-General, Sir Henry J. Lightfoot-Boston on March 21, 1967. Two days later, however, his own officers overruled his authority and toppled him. Under the chairmanship of Col. Andrew Juxon-Smith, seven officers-- five military and two police officers-- formed a National Reformation Council (NRC). The Commissioner of Police, Mr. William Leigh, became the Deputy Chairman.

Their aims, according to them, were to restore the dwindling economy, end corruption, and then return power to a civilian rule. At first, these seemed legitimate to the populace. But as months passed by without signs of righting the wrongs and/or relinquishing power, popular feelings, especially within the army ranks, turned against them. On April 18, 1968, a group of private soldiers, aided by some of their Non-Commissioned Officers (NCO's), in what was tagged a "coup of sergeant's," arrested the officers and restored the country to a civilian rule. APC took power on April 26, 1968 on the strength of the majority it had won at the election the year before, with Siaka Stevens as the Prime Minister. SLPP suddenly became an opposition party. On July 30, 1970, Brigadier Juxon-Smith was sentenced to death for the coup.

In March 1971, an Army Commander, Brig. John Bangura, was involved in another coup attempt. About two known attempts were made to assassinate Stevens to no avail. Bangura and three other officers were found guilty on the attempted coup and were subsequently executed. In April 1971, a Bill was passed in the parliament declaring Sierra Leone a Republic and Stevens became an executive president, with Sorie I. Koroma as prime minister and vice-president. In a referendum in June 1978 following the House of Representatives approval in May

1978, Sierra Leone became a one-party state.

As Siaka Stevens was preparing his awaited retirement from public life, and ignoring the claims of his two vice-presidents, Sorie Koroma and Francis Minah, he chose as his successor, the head of the armed forces, Maj. Gen. Joseph Saidu Momoh who was an appointed member of the House of Representatives and a cabinet member.

During the APC convention in August 1985, Momoh was unanimously elected president-designate and leader of APC. This was officially endorsed in October by a nation-wide presidential election. In November 1985, Momoh was formally installed as president. Stevens, however, retained the chairmanship of the APC. He died on May 29, 1988 peacefully at his home, in the arms of his wife, Rebecca Stevens.

Somalia: The Republic of Somalia, consisting of the former British Somaliland and the former Trust Territory of Somalia, with capital at Mogadishu, gained her independence on July 1, 1960. Mr. Aden Abdullah Osman, President of the Somalia (Trust Territory) Legislative Assembly, on the same day of the independence, was proclaimed the provisional president of the Republic, at a joint meeting of the representatives of the two former territories. On July 12,

1960, Dr. Abdelrashid Ali Shermarke, a member of the former Somalia Legislative Assembly and a leading Somalia Youth League (SYL), was chosen as the first Prime Minister by the president.

Dr. Abdelrashid Shermarke was from the Darod clan, while President Osman came from Hawiye.

As a result of a new election, Mr. Abdirizak Hadji Hussein was appointed Prime Minister on June 14, 1964. On July 13, 1964, the government was defeated on its first conference vote because Hussein was regarded as pro-west.

On June 10, 1967, Dr. Shermarke was elected President of the Republic by the National Assembly in a secret ballot, which gave him 73 votes against 50 for President Osman. He chose Muhammed Haji Ibrahim Egal, a northerner of the Isaq clan as Prime Minister. However, on October 15, 1969, as a result of a factional quarrel, President Shermarke was assassinated by a member of the police force, who was subsequently sentenced to death on October 8, 1970.

On October 20, 1970, Hadji Musa Boghor was nominated President over Sheik Mukhtar Mohammed Hussein who was an acting president. Nonetheless, on October 21, 1970, Army commanders, supported by the police, seized power. The National Assembly was dissolved, the constitution suspended, and cabinet members arrested. The Supreme Court was also abolished. The leader of the coup, Gen. Mohammed Siyad Barreh, Commander-in-Chief of the Armed Forces, was named the chairman of the 25-member Supreme Revolutionary Council (SRC). The council announced that their action was to preserve democracy and justice and to eliminate corruption and tribalism. To symbolize all these, the country was renamed Somali Democratic Republic.

Although titular Head of State when he initially came to power, President Siyad Barreh later became popular, due to his social agenda. His guiding motto was "tribalism divides, socialism unites." The mother tongue replaced three foreign languages -- English, Italian and Arabic -- as the official written medium. This made literacy possible for a great number of people who could have been locked out of political and governmental processes.

In May 1986, Siyad Barreh was seriously injured in a motor accident. He was, however, flown to Riyadh, Saudi Arabia for medical treatment. Lt. Gen. Mohammed Ali Samater, the Minister of Defence, took control during this period, along with the President's son-in-law, Brig. Gen. Ahmed Suleyman Abdulle, who was the Minister of External Affairs. President Barreh later recovered but had to be in a convalescence period for a few months.

Togo, with its capital at Lome, and an official language as French, gained her independence as a Republic on April 27, 1960, under the premiership of Sylvanus Olympio who had held the Prime Minister position since April, 1958.

Olympio was elected President of the new Republic on April 9, 1961. Togo, later, became a one-party state; thus, problems emerged.

Olympio was the leader of Comite de l'unite togolaise (CUT), while his arch rival, Nicolas Grunitzky, his brother-in-law, led parti de l'unite togolaise, (PUT). Despite Olympio's successful economic management of the nation, he faced considerable political opposition, particularly from Grunitzky who had gone into exile in Paris.

Sylvanus Olympio was assassinated on January 13, 1963, in a coup d'etat led by Sergeant (later General) Etienne (Gnassingbe) Eyadema, who quickly invited Grunitzky to return from exile to form a provisional government. He formed the government on January 17, 1963. In a referendum administered on May 5, 1963, a new constitution was approved and Grunitzky was confirmed as President and Antoine Meatchi, head of Union des chefs et des populations du nord, as vice president.

An attempted coup by Olympio's supporters led by Dr. Noe Kutuklui in November 1966, citing corruption in the government, failed. However, on January 13, 1967, at the fourth anniversary of Olympio's death, Lt. Col. Eyadema, who was then the Army Chief of Staff, seized power, this time in a bloodless coup, citing danger of a civil war. He dismissed the civilian government and Grunitzky went back into exile in Paris where he finally died in 1969.

In January 1972, a referendum was held to approve if Eyadema should remain as president. This garnered an overwhelming yes. In 1974, he started the campaign of "authenticity" in which foreign personal, surname, place and/or street names were abandoned for local ones, in accordance with Mobutu Sese Seko of Zaire's preaching. He changed his own name from Etienne to Gnassingbe. The two main national languages, Ewe and Kabiye, were introduced into state schools, and later to replace French as the language of education. As expected, there were initial conflicts of interest between the state and the Roman Catholic church over the campaign. But the state prevailed anyway.

In November 1979, in what was known as the third Republic, a new constitution for elective presidential system was discussed and approved. On December 30, 1979, Eyadema, the sole candidate, was elected with nearly 100% of the vote. Of late, Eyadema and his secret police and supporters are being accused of torturing political prisoners and dissenters. The government prevented an attempt by the Amnesty International, a civil rights organisation based in London, from sending its representatives to Togo in 1986. But Eyadema projects to the world an image of a popular and fair president.

Uganda, with its capital in Kampala, gained her independence on October 9, 1962 under the premiership of Dr. Apollo Milton Obote. When the country became a republic on October 4, 1963, the government was formed by the coalition of Uganda People's Congress (UPC) led by Dr. Apollo Milton Obote and Kabaka Yekka (KY), or literally, the "King Alone," led by the Kabaka, Sir Edward Frederick Mutesa II.

Due to the coalition, the Kabaka (king) of Buganda, Sir Edward Frederick Mutesa II, was elected President, Sir William Wilberforce Nadiope, the Kyabazinga (traditional ruler) of Busoga, Vice President, and Dr. Obote, the Prime Minister.

In 1966, Daudi Ocheng, an Acholi with close links to Buganda, introduced a motion in the National Assembly to suspend Col. Idi Amin Dada from duty and investigate the alleged gold smuggling by Obote, Felix Onama (the Minister of

Defence) and Adoko Nekyon (a cousin of Obote). The gold smuggling was a secret involvement, since 1964, in aiding anti-Tshombe rebels in Congo (now Zaire) with the help of Tanzania and Zambia. Uganda provided the facilities for the smuggling of ivory and gold to purchase armaments and a transit route for the rebels' supplies. Amin was in charge of marketing the smuggled gold. The motion was approved almost unanimously.

A commission of inquiry which was to reject the charges was constituted by Obote. Thus, Obote's planned civilian coup. He sent the second-in-command of the army, then Col. Idi Amin Dada, on leave with pay as a result of the allegation against Obote's government. Armed with the "not-guilty" verdict by the Commission of Inquiry, Obote ordered the arrest of five ministers of his government, suspended the existing 1962 constitution, deposed the President, and all executive powers were vested on himself.

In 1967, Uganda became a new republic with executive presidency. An abolition of the four hereditary kingdoms were made on June 9, 1967. A new constitution, quickly written and approved, conferred executive presidency on Obote; thus, the extinction of Kabaka's political powers. The new republic with executive presidency, officially took effect on September 8,

1967. The Kabaka went into exile in England. A one-party system of government was later adopted.

As Obote left for a Commonwealth conference in Singapore, on January 25, 1971, through activities promoted by Britain and Israel's Mossad, Major Gen. (later Field Marshal) Idi Amin Dada, seized power. It was alleged that Britain, disturbed by Obote's leftist stance and his contacts with the Soviet Union, and Israel, by Obote's blocking of support for the Southern Sudanese guerrillas, orchestrated the Amin coup.

On February 2, 1971, Amin declared himself Head-of-State, and on February 21, he became the President of Uganda by proclamation. Gen. Amin's regime was officially recognized by Britain on February 5, 1971, and quickly followed by Israel. Amin promised to return the country to a civil rule in five years. The coup, at the time, was greeted by an enthusiastic crowd without knowing where the turbulent wave of events would take them. He moved ahead in releasing some political prisoners and arranged to have the remains of the late Kabaka, Mutesa II, flown from London for a lavish reburial at Kasubi.

As time went by, Amin embarked in the massacre of the troops and police that supported Obote. He established the State Research Bureau (SRB), headquartered in Nakasero in central Kampala, to provide intelligence on the civilian population. He used this intelligence to slaughter the people.

Among prominent persons Amin and his regime killed, directly or indirectly, included a Roman Catholic priest, Reverend Father Clement Kiggundu, Editor of the Catholic Newspaper known as Munno, Benedicto Kiwanuka, a Chief Justice of Uganda, whom Idi Amin ordered (to be) killed. (He was Uganda's first Chief Minister and the leader of the Democratic Party.) His body was never recovered, although it was well known that he was killed while still in detention at Makindye Military Barracks in Kampala after being abducted from his High Court office. The Anglican Archbishop Janan Luwum, whose death along with the government Ministers -- Colonel Erinago Oryema, Amin's Minister of Land Resources and Charles Oboth Ofumbi, the Minister of Internal Affairs -- Amin ludicrously claimed resulted from a car accident. Self-made millionaire, Michael Kawalya Kaggwa, whose body was allegedly thrown into a blazing Mercedes Benz car; his body burnt beyond recognition; and many others.

Of all Amin's atrocities, the death of the Archbishop Janan Luwum created a world uproar. Idi Amin's secret intelligence claimed that they discovered some arms in the residence of the

Archbishop at the church's headquarters in Namirembe, Kampala. Unfortunately for the church, the alleged discovery of the weapons was at the height of the government's suspicion and/or detection of a plot by the Ugandan exiles based in Tanzania, to topple the treacherous Amin and his government.

The Cabinet Ministers -- Col. Erinayo Oryema and Charles Oboth Ofumbi-- were mysteriously linked to the alleged plot or its collaboration.

The bodies of most victims of the State terror were thrown into Kafu River. It was said in Uganda that when a person failed to find a relation or friend picked up by the mischievous secret police, he only needed to visit the river's banks on Kampala-Jinja road. What a shameful terror to mankind.

Amin's arrogance and despotism excelled any one in recent memory, except, to a certain degree, the Obote's second coming. He forced some British diplomats in his country to push his Presidential limousine while he relaxed inside it. He collaborated with the Palestine Liberation Organization (PLO), in high-jacking an Israeli Airline with several people on board in 1976. Israel dealt him a blow by a stealth and clandestine operation to rescue her citizens at Entebbe Airport. That famous Entebbe operation dramatically reduced

Idi Amin's egocentrism. He began to realize that irrespective of all his powers, he was still vulnerable. To the advantage of Israel, an Israeli company constructed the Entebbe Airport for Uganda.

Idi Amin conferred himself with all the titles one can think of in this world. He awarded himself his country's Military Cross, Distinguished Service Order, and Victory Cross. When that did not seem sufficient, he created his own award, politically called Conqueror of British Empire (CBE), which he bestowed himself as the first recipient. It must be remembered though, that Britain helped put him in power. What an irony!

As there was no more military hono(u)rs left, he turned to academia, forcing a Ugandan university -- Makerere University -- to award him a doctor of literature (or letters), otherwise known as D. Litt. By the time he was run out of Uganda by the Tanzanian forces which supported Obote's bid to come back, his name and the acronyms had become Alhaji, Dr., Field Marshal Idi Amin Dada, "President-for-Life," with several wives and over 22 children.

Ugandan forces, by the order of Amin, had earlier aggressively crossed into the Tanzanian border. This forced President Julius Nyerere to determine that he would run Amin out of the country by all possible means. In late April 1979, Amin escaped to Libya and subsequently into Saudi Arabia where he agreed to be apolitical. Soldiers loyal to him crossed to Zaire and Sudanese borders.

After Amin, a compromise government was formed. Yusufu Lule, who was more of an academic than a politician, was sworn in on April 13, 1979 as President. His inexperience and straight-forward commitment to restore power of Buganda, cost him his post. On June 19, 1979, he was voted out by the National Consultative Committee (NCC) of Uganda's National Liberation Front. The former Attorney General, Godfrey Binaisa was named in his stead. Lule moved to Tanzania again.

Binaisa's leadership proved to be as ineffective as Lule. Like Lule, he tried to bypass the authority of NCC which was the de facto decision maker. He was manoeuvred by Dr. Apollo Milton Obote and Paul Muwanga to dismiss the Minister of Defence, Yoweri Museveni, in 1979, who, by a twist of fate, would later rule Uganda. This action, widely viewed as a mistake, gravely weakened his position with NCC. His subsequent attempt to dismiss Muwanga, the Minister of Internal Affairs, and David Oyite-Ojok without success, completely brought his downfall. Between May 9-11, 1980, nobody was sure who was running the country. However, on

May 12, the power was assumed by the Ugandan National Liberation Front (UNLF) military commission, under the chairmanship of Paul Muwanga, supported by David Oyite-Ojok and Tito Okello, with Yoweri Museveni as vice-chairman.

After the triumphant return of Dr. Obote to the Southwestern town of Mushenyi on May 27, 1980, the scheduled general election of September 30, was rescheduled for December 10, 1980, to accommodate Obote.

After the controversial election, Dr. Obote was proclaimed President with Muwanga as Vice President and Minister of Defence, and Otema Allimadi, the former External Affairs Minister, as Prime Minister on December 15, 1980.

President Obote seized the opportunity to exercise vengeance on the citizens that supported Idi Amin, not only during the tumultuous years he reigned, but during his forced exile also. During the course of his exorcism, he became worse than Amin. It was alleged in the U.S. Congress in mid-1984 that about 100,000 civilians had already been killed under Obote's administration. This led to a divided army loyalty.

On July 27, 1985, General Tito Okello deposed Obote in a military coup d'etat. However, Gen. Okello's regime did not make it up to a year because of the continued unrest in the country.

The National Resistance Army (NRA), led by Yoweri Museveni and others, formed a strong opposition to the government. On January 27, 1986, Kampala, the capital, fell to an NRA Army which included children. Law and order were restored in the capital. On January 29, 1986, Museveni was sworn in as President. He formed a cabinet that almost included other factions of that troubled society. He has outwitted other guerilla attacks to overthrow his government, including that of Priestess Alice Lakwena and her Holy Spirit Movement that used voodoo, which she claimed, with only oil and stones, the government's guns could be neutralised.

She later found out that oil and stone do not mix with water and gun, as the government's heavy-duty ammunition pierced through most members of the Movement to perpetual extermination.

Zaire, formerly Congo Kinshasa, with capital at Kinshasa and French as the official language, gained independence on June 30, 1960. On June 23, 1960, Mr. Patrice Lumumba who was elected Prime Minister, formed a government comprising virtually all political parties but Kalonji wing of Mouvement National de Congolaise (MNC). Joseph Kasavubu, the leader of the Abako, was elected President (Head of State) by the parliament on June 24, 1960.

A few days after the independence, July 5-6, 1960, a riot erupted by the army officials who were protesting low rank and low pay. They started the rioting against the Belgians and Europeans. Following the crisis, the chief of staff of the Army, Gen. Emile Janssens was replaced and Lumumba promoted and appointed Congolese citizens in the high military posts, including the appointment of a 30-year old, Joseph-Desire Mobutu, as the Army Chief of Staff.

During the crisis that forced some Congolese to flee their country, Belgian troops intervened to protect their nationals. In the process, on July 11, 1960, as Lumumba appeal(l)ed to the United Nations for the help of military specialists to assist in the reorganisation of the embattled Congolese military forces, Mr. Moise Tshombe, late the same day, announced Katanga's (now Shaba) independence. South Kasai also decided to secede too. Katanga was one of the regions in the Congo. A civil war commenced, followed by a disagreement between the Prime Minister and the Head of State.

The Head of State used the advantage of the (Constitutional) article in the Loi fondamentale to dismiss Lumumba as the Prime Minister. He appointed Joseph

Ileo, the President of the Senate, in his place. Patrice Lumumba immediately declared that he was still the Prime Minister and that Kasavubu was a "traitor" and was no longer the Head of State. He turned to the parliament to remove him officially. The parliament voted in favour of removing Kasavubu but lacked the constitutional quorum, thus, invalidating the eventual outcome.

As the conflict continued, Col. Joseph-Desire Mobutu, the Army Chief of Staff who previously appeared to support Lumumba, on September 14, 1960, announced that the Army had taken over the Supreme power, and that all political activities, including the two rival governments of Ileo and Lumumba, would be suspended until December 13, 1960. He appointed a "College of Commissioners" or college des commissaire generaux who were mainly young university graduates and students, to run the government.

The relationship between Col. Mobutu and the United Nations Organization (U. N. O.), was strained, because he could not arrest Lumumba who was under the protection of the United Nations forces at the Prime Minister's official residence from October 10 through November 27, 1960.

Col. Mobutu's troops captured Lumumba on December 1, 1960, after he escaped from Leopoldville on November 27, with the aim of reaching a group of his supporters under the leadership of Mr. Antoine Gizenga, Gen. Victor Lundula and Bernard Salumu, who had established a Lumumbist centre of power at Stanleyville (now Kisangani), capital of the Eastern province. Lumumba was transferred from Thysville prison to Katanga during January 1961. The Katangan Minister of Interior, Godefroid Munongo, announced thereafter, that Lumumba had been assassinated by the villagers near Kolwezi, 210 miles northwest of the then Elizabethville, capital of Katanga.

An investigation on Lumumba's death by the United Nations, published on November 14, 1961, said that "most likely" the former Prime Minister had been shot, with two companions, by a Belgian officer in the presence of Mr. Tshombe (his enemy) and other Katangan leaders. Tshombe later described the report as "completely false."

Dr. Patrick Francis Wilmot, a former Lecturer of Sociology at Ahmadu Bello University, Zaria, in Nigeria, in his article, "Africa Must Unite," written from his London residence, in The African Concord Magazine of May 10, 1988, stressed that, "Patrice Lumumba was tortured, killed, cut into pieces and dissolved in the acid vats of the Belgian Union Miniere Corporation." Dr. Wilmot was a Jamaican born but American educated, who was unceremoniously deported to London on March 10, 1988 by the Nigerian military government after lecturing in a Nigerian University for about 18 years.

As Col. Mobutu ruled with decree, he appointed Justine-Marie Bomboko, previously Minister of Foreign Affairs under Lumumba's government, as the chairman of the College des commissaire generaux.

Shortly before Lumumba's death, President Kasavubu, on February 9, 1961, issued a decree establishing a Central Congolese Government under the premiership of Joseph Ileo, while at the same time, dissolving the college of commissioners. Col. Mobutu, already on January 22, 1961, had been named the Commander-in-Chief of the Congolese National Army.

Meanwhile, the U.N. Secretary-General, Dr. Dag Hammarskjold, was replaced on November 3, 1961, by U Thant after the death of Dr. Hammarskjold on an air crash on September 17, 1961, on his way to Elizabethville (now Lumumbashi), the capital of Katanga.

The civil war eventually ended by the help of the U.N. forces in which most African nations, including Ghana and Nigeria, participated. Major General J. T. U. Aguiyi-Ironsi of Nigeria was among the participants (commander) in that peace-keeping force. After the war, the Congo started going through a reconciliation process.

After spending over a year in Paris and Madrid, Spain, Tshombe, on June 24, 1964, announced that he was going to Leopoldville (now Kinshasa), "at the invitation of the Central Government," to work together, in order to achieve "effective and immediate reconciliation and liberation of the country from misery and anarchy." President Kasavubu, on July 6, 1964, officially invited Tshombe who arrived on June 26, to form a cabinet. The cabinet was sworn in on July 10, 1964.

After a short political romance, misunderstanding cropped in between the President and Tshombe. The President dismissed him and appointed Evariste Kimba, who could not muster a majority support in the newly constituted Assembly, formed as a result of the August 1, 1964 constitution. Instead of appointing a new premier, President Kasavubu reappointed Kimba. As the antagonistic situation could not be ameliorated, Gen. Joseph-Desire Mobutu, on November 25, 1965, to neutralize the two sides, deposed the government and assumed the presidency. By proclamation, he appointed his right-hand man, Col. (later General) Leonard Mulamba as Prime Minister.

On April 6, 1966, he divided the country into 12 provinces instead of the 21 established in 1962-63. Thereafter, he started an "authenticity" campaign. From June 30, 1966, several towns whose names were of European origin were renamed, such as Leopoldville to Kinshasa, Elizabethville to Lumumbashi, Stanleyville to Kisangani, etc. His name was changed from Joseph-Desire Mobutu to Mobutu Sese Seko and his country, from Congo to Zaire in January 1972. All personal names and surnames of the citizens were forced to change to local names.

As the country adopted a new constitution of presidentialism, which was not enforced till three years after its approval, because its sole candidate, Mobutu, was less than 40 years -- the minimum age required to run for presidency -- Mobutu took the reign of office. Moise Tshombe was eventually charged for high treason and sentenced to death. He, however, died in Algiers, Algeria, of heart failure on June 29, 1969.

Mobutu's one-party system, mouvement populaire de la Revolution (MPR), became absolute in the country. In the first week of October 1988, Pieter W. Botha of South Africa, paid an official visit to Mobutu in Zaire. Mobutu was alleged to have said on October 3, 1988, that he pleaded and received assurance for the release of the imprisoned anti-apartheid activist Nelson Mandela, from Botha. He said he would return the visit at a future date. After the visit, he probably would not have a country to return.

ANALYSIS OF COUP D'ETAT IN AFRICA.
Reasons given for military intervention in the African continent, vary greatly. Some mutineers and coup lords, alleged unaccountability of politicians, coupled with nepotism, embezzlement, tribalism and indifference to the welfare of the masses, as their reasons for infringement into the political process.

In addition to the aforementioned, some cite absolute power mania and one-party state system. Wrote Col. (later Gen.) A. A. Afrifa, on his book titled, The Ghana Coup, 24th February, 1966, "A coup d'etat is the last resort in the range of means whereby an unpopular government may be overthrown. But in our case where there was no constitutional means of offering a political opposition to one-party government, the Armed Forces were automatically made to become the official opposition to the government."

Economic and technological stagnation equally had been cited as another reason. But how can the developed world, which in most cases precipitate the instability in the developing countries, transfer technology or inject capital into those politically unstable world. This is paradoxical, isn't it?

Wrote William F. Gutteridge in his book, The Military in African Politics, "A feature of African political development has been the high degree of spontaneity, unpredictability, and general volatility of political reactions at all levels."

The fact remains that the western world and other developed world are the culprit of African political instability and economic malaise, followed by the third world ignorance, which allows tribalism and clannishness to cloud, overcome and/or overwhelm the general and future good and stability of their countries in particular, and the African continent in general.

The Western World's culpability can be briefly cited in some coups in Africa. The American Central Intelligence Agency (CIA) and the British High Commission, were implicated in the assassination of Gen. Murtala Muhammed of Nigeria; Britain and Israel were implicated in putting Idi Amin into power; Belgium was implicated, at least by the United Nations' investigation (with the CIA), in the destabilization of Congo (now Zaire) and the humiliating assassination of Patrice Lumumba, to mention just a few.

American Central Intelligence Agency failed in the Bay of Pigs of Cuba (an attempt to topple Fidel Castro through the use of 1,200 dissident Cubans) during President John Fitzgerald Kennedy's administration in April 1961. The late Robert Francis Kennedy, his brother's administration Attorney General, who was equally assassinated on June 6, 1968 by the bullet of Sirhan Bishara Sirhan, at the Ambassador Hotel in Los Angeles, California, in a book titled, "Robert Kennedy: In His Own Words," implied that the erroneous invasion of Cuba through the Bay of Pigs, was part of learning on the job.

Wrote Joe K. Crews of Dallas in the Dallas Times Herald of Wednesday, April 18, 1984, titled, "Goodwill Excursion by the CIA," "Perhaps the most mendacious and Machiavellian of any U.S. institution, the CIA appears to be sowing its seed of horror once again. Its persistence is matched only the Reagan administration's disingenuousness about its activity.

"The CIA has become an Orwellian reality. Most recently, after rewriting history in Chile (1970-73), the CIA has attempted the assassination of Jamaica's democratically elected Michael Manley (1976-79); it attempted a coup to overthrow Grenada's Maurice Bishop (1980); it provided the economic basis for the electoral defeat by Dominica's

Eugenia Charles of Oliver Seraphine (1980); it assassinated Guyanan opposition leader Walter Rodney (1980); it implemented anti-Sandinista sabotage and terrorist incursions into Nicaragua (1980-current); it organized the Guatemalan military coup to overthrow Anibal Guevara (1980); it organized the Bolivian military coup to overthrow Torrelio (1982) and on three occasions, it attempted to overthrow the Suriname Government of Col. Bouterse.

"To continue with its Latin American goodwill tour, the CIA is now placing mines in Nicaragua's Atlantic and Pacific harbo(u)rs . . ." It must be noted that President Salvador Allende of Chile died during the 1973 coup.

The Dallas Morning News editorial of Friday, July 29, 1988, highlighted that "Wilson Administration futilely chased Pancho Villa across Northern Mexico in 1916; Eisenhower administration effectively overthrew Guatemala's Jacob Arbenz Guzman and Iran's Mohammed Mossadegh in the 1950's."

These are just Latin American and Asian examples. Any African leader that fully stands tall and vigorously fights for African interest, most of the time is either assassinated, or the economic viability of his country is sabotaged, thus, a good ground for coup d' etat. The architects of African saboteurs are not only American CIA; No. 10 Downing Street, London, French Intelligence, Soviet K. G. B. (Komitet Gosudarstvennoi Bezopasnosti, that is, Committee For State Security), as well as Israel's effective Mossad Intelligence are not exempted.

Ignorance, which fosters tribal intolerance in most African countries, is an enormous stigma that will continue to pest Africa and the rest of the developing nations, unless a drastic mass education is undertaken to enlighten the people.

Even the so-called educated people or elites, hardly make things easy either, since they already have on their mind that nothing can be done about it. Nigeria, unfortunately, is such a country. The geographical names of Eastern Region, Northern Region, and Western Region in Nigeria that instantly depicted which tribe a person or state belonged to had for long been dismantled. Different regimes had tried to remove the removable and disbandable vestiges of tribalism to no avail. Tribalism is the most single canker worm that continues to eat into the fabric of Nigerian unity in particular, and Africa and developing world's unity in general today.

It is up to the African leaders to chart a new and enviable course for their respective nations and continent.

Absolutism corrupts absolutely, and suppression of political dissent, as A. A. Afrifa wrote, causes discontent, hence, an alternative to an existing government, whether military or otherwise. As Major Gen. Sanni Abacha of Nigeria said on June 4, 1988, no law can stop coups d'etat (in Nigeria) except "good government." The meaning of "good government," however, is open for interpretation, especially when it is said by a military coup-lord.

The military coups in Africa are due to different reasons at different times and at different countries. Some stage a coup just to grab power; some overthrow a government in order to enrich themselves; a few participate in reactionaryism, while others act in varying degrees of true reform and fairness. Some military coup lords, like Mobuta Sese Seko of Zaire, although with good intentions then, entrenched themselves in the seat of power without any possibility of letting others to effectively contribute their fair share, while the repugnant overthrow and unceremonious assassination of able and charismatic leaders like Captain Thomas Sankara of Burkina Faso, by a feeble-minded idiot like Captain Blaise Compaore (who knows when he would promote himself to General), makes coup d'etat of any form totally nonsensical and condemnable.

According to the review of the book,

"How can Africa Survive?" written by Jennifer Seymour Whitaker, Business Week Magazine (USA) of August 8, 1988 wrote, ". . . venal leaders, such as Zaire's President Mobutu Sese Seko, who allegedly has personal fortune of $4.5 billion, dreamed of Swiss bank accounts as well as steel mills, and looted state coffers."

Said Patrick F. Wilmot in his lecture at the Oxford University in October 1988, as reported by the African Concord of December 12, 1988, "For desperate citizens, the green khaki is no longer a symbol of hope but the green of the plagues of locust that ravaged and lay waste. The corruption of the civilians, one of the ostensible reasons for which they were overthrown, pales into insignificance next to the kleptocracy of Mobutu (Sese Seko).

"The debt of the country is five billion dollars, and coincidentally, that is the estimate of how much Mobutu and his family have stolen from Zaire. He owns no less than seven chateaus in Belgium and France, as well as palatial estates and residences in Spain, Italy and Switzerland. He owns buildings in the Ivory Coast, presidential mansions in each of the country's eight provinces, and a palace in his home province. No one knows how much he has in Swiss banks and he has exclusive use or ownership of numerous ships, jet planes (including a Boeing 747), at least 51 Mercedes, and so on. His plantation, CELZA, is the third largest employer in Zaire and produces about one sixth of the country's agricultural exports . . . (He also owns) shares in every foreign company in the country, in the banks, and (takes commissions) of 5% of the country's mineral production paid to his overseas accounts. Thirty per cent of the country's operating budget flows through the President's office with no further accounting," he continued.

Dr. Wilmot who was once a sociology lecturer at one of the Nigerian universities, stressed that, "Like other African generals and field marshals, Mobutu has taken good care of himself. As their people sink deeper and deeper into poverty, they acquire more and more exclusive properties in Europe, and siphon the little remaining wealth into coded bank accounts. Their wives shop in the most exclusive boutiques in Europe and America, and their children attend the most exclusive schools in Switzerland. And with their austerity programmes, focused exclusively on extracting the last ounce of surplus from the poor, they punish the victims of their own crimes."

Beyond Dr. Wilmot's account of Mobutu's ill-gotten wealth, who knows how much the American CIA is paying him for his accessory to the destabilization of the Front Line States, particularly

Angola. This is not impossible. After all, it was of recent that everyone learned that General Manuel Anthonio Noriega of Panama had been on the secret CIA payroll for several years, earning as much as $200,000.00 per annum. This is the exact amount, at this writing, that a U.S.A. president earns as salary per annum. And the racist South African President Pieter W. Botha, who is now ailing (he suffered a stroke in late January 1989 and now is virtually replaced by the Education Minister Frederik W. de Klerk, 52, who is also conservative and a party leader of the populous Transvaal Province), in October 1988, paid Mobutu an official state visit. There is no doubt that any such financial remuneration to Mobutu or any of those African "stooges" by the Central Intelligence Agency would be "classified," until he/they fall out of favour as Noriega did in 1986.

Mobutu Sese Seko's stealth and kleptocracy are in sharp contrast with the persona and patriotism of Col. Moamer al Kadhafi (some write it as Muammar Qaddafi or Gadhafi) of Libya. Again wrote Dr. P. F. Wilmot in the African Concord of December 12, 1988, this time about Gadhafi: "Despite his erratic nature and unpredictability of some of his actions, and the confusion of his thinking, one can say that Gadhafi's heart is in the right place, even if his head sometimes is not. He is not a thief and has genuinely attempted to use the wealth of his country for the benefit of his people. Even though he lacks Nasser's (of Egypt) vision, intelligence, and emotional stability, he has tried to keep the Pan-Arab idea alive. He had the courage to stand up to American aggression when the interests and the sovereignty of the Libyan people were convened."

It is widely believed that if Libya's population is to be one-fifth the size of Nigeria's 100 million-plus population -- the most populous nation in Africa -- Libya could have vied for a permanent position in the United Nations Organisation's Security Council. Libya's population is less than three million with rich mineral resources. And luckily for her, she has able, dedicated, and incorruptible leader like Col. Gadhafi, irrespective of his erratic and sometimes unconscionable behaviour.

Military coup is supposed to be a corrective measure to redirect the nation's course. And military regime is, by all purposes, supposed to be transitional of not more than three years. Any military government that stays in power beyond two and a half years, corrupts itself like the old institution which it tries to correct. The reason behind this is that beyond two and a half years or three years, the old guards infiltrate by either hook or crook, into the military wall. And as the military embraces politics, perhaps inadvertently, to stay in power, in addition to the exercise of absolute power, it embezzles and enriches itself. The momentum it once had, dissipates into oblivion, and the citizens will once again call for a change of guard and/or return to an alternative system.

No military government, no matter how civilized it may be, wants any criticism of any kind. That was perhaps the reason Chief Chris Okoli, Editor of the Newbreed Magazine in Nigeria was arrested by the State Security Service (SSS) agents, on Tuesday, February 7, 1989 for his magazine's article, "A Harvest of Generals," questioning the recent military promotions in Nigeria while the citizens were suffering austerity measures. Nigeria now has more generals than any time in history. And most of these promotions were/are during a military rule. It is believed that Nigeria has more generals than most countries of the world. At this writing, it has 23 generals in "active duty," all of them promoted during peace time.

It is only in a few occasions that a military regime has done its job effectively and leave politicking to the politicians in Africa. Armed forces in the actual sense are meant to defend the nation and not to rule. This basic function is now being reneged by the military turned politicians, or should they be called militico-polity. Military is for taking orders from the civilian ruled state, and not vice versa. May be they need to be sent back to the basic military school for reorientation. But who will bell the cat as they are the ones who carry the guns?

It is now more evident that the availability of arms, their use and/or threat of their use, are in part the sine qua non of military intervention in Africa and elsewhere. Nonetheless, the politicians who turn state treasury into their coffers must be taught bitter lessons, and swiftly too. Any lackadaisical adjudication of justice, mitigates the seriousness and atrociousness of their crime against the citizens and the state.

Perhaps, it is true that those who make peaceful resolution impossible, make violent revolution inevitable. Thus, the politicians or the military juntas who stay put in the seat of power, could end up where they started, or worse, stoop further into the bottom of the valley. Then, power, which usually has two faces -- to do good or evil -- will continue its journey and finally rests on the best alternative of the time. While the situation might be begging for answers, life, as usual, will go on.

PART THREE

* * *

RIP VAN WINKLE AS AFRICA

Rip Van Winkle, a fictional character created by Washington Irving, slept for 20 years and awoke to find that the entire world around him had become completely different. He was amazed at the new environment, confused by all that had taken place while he slept, and at a loss to understand how to adjust to all the changes.

In the case of many African nations, they slept far more than twenty years. The continent itself slept for over a century without adapting to new changes, including the power structure in the world. That was among the reasons some of her children were humiliated and enslaved to far away continents. Those left behind became divided and suspicious of one another. The irony of this is that Africa was where Homo sapiens (first human species) originated. That is no wonder they are economically and technologically behind. Hence corruption emerged when some woke up from their slumber.

There must be peace first in any

nation before (it) plans for the future. Who knows what the future holds. As you read on, you will see that there are turbulent waters ahead and why they are sailable if foreign manipulation of Africans can be contained.

* * *

SUMMARY OF ORGANISATION OF AFRICAN UNITY (OAU) CHARTER

The Organization was founded on May 25, 1963 to promote unity and solidarity among African nations.

Address: P. O. Box 3243
           Addis Ababa, Ethiopia

Phone: 4 74 80

<u>Article I</u>: The Establishment of the Organization of African Unity: The organization is to include the continental African States, Madagascar, and other islands surrounding Africa.

<u>Article II</u>: Aims of the OAU:

1. To promote unity and solidarity among African States.
2. To intensify and coordinate efforts to improve living standards in Africa.
3. To defend the sovereignty, territorial integrity and independence of African States.

4. To eradicate all forms of colonialism from Africa.
5. To promote international cooperation in keeping with the charter of the United Nations.

Article III: The member states should adhere to the principles of sovereignty, non-interference in internal affairs of member states, respect for territorial integrity, peaceful settlement of disputes, condemnation of political subversion, dedication to the emancipation of dependent African territories, and international non-alignment.

ARTICLE IV: Each independent sovereign African state shall be entitled to become a member of the organization.

ARTICLE V: All member states shall have equal rights and duties.

ARTICLE VI: All member states shall observe scrupulously the principles laid down in Article III.

ARTICLE VII: Establishment of the Assembly of Heads of State and Government, the Council of Ministers, the General Secretariat, and the Commission of Mediation, Conciliation and Arbitration.

ARTICLE VIII-XI: The Assembly of Heads of State and Government coordinates policies, and reviews the structure of the organization.

ARTICLE XII-XV: The Council of Ministers shall prepare the conference of the Assembly, and coordinate inter-African cooperation. All resolutions shall be by a simple majority.

ARTICLE XVI-XVIII: The General Secretariat. The administrative Secretary-General and his staff shall not seek or receive instructions from any government or other authority external to the Organization. They are international officials responsible only to the Organization.

ARTICLE XIX: Commission of Mediation, Conciliation and Arbitration. A separate protocol concerning the composition and nature of this commission shall be regarded as an integral part of the charter.

ARTICLE XX-XXII: A specialized Commission shall be established, composed of Ministers or other officials designated by the Member Governments. Their regulations shall be laid down by the Council of Ministers.

ARTICLE XXIII: The budget shall be prepared by the Secretary-General, and approved by the Council of Ministers. Contributions shall be in accordance with the scale of assessment of the United Nations. No member shall pay more than 20% of the total yearly amount.

ARTICLE XXIV: Texts of the Charter in African languages, English and French, shall be equally authentic. Instruments of ratification shall be deposited with the Government of Ethiopia.

ARTICLE XXV: The charter shall come into force on receipt by the Government of Ethiopia of the instruments of ratification of two-thirds of the signatory states.

ARTICLE XXVI: The charter shall be registered with the secretariat of the United Nations.

ARTICLE XXVII: The questions of interpretation shall be settled by a two-thirds majority vote in the Assembly of Heads of States and government.

ARTICLE XXVIII: Admission of new independent African States to the organization shall be decided by a simple majority of the Member

States.

ARTICLE XXIX-XXXIII: The working languages of the organization shall be African languages, English and French. The Secretary-General may accept gifts and bequests to the Organization, subject to the approval of the Council of Ministers. The Council of Ministers shall establish privileges and immunities to be accorded to the personnel of the secretariat in the territories of the Member states. A State wishing to withdraw from the Organization, must give a year's written notice to the secretariat. The charter may only be amended after consideration by all Member states and by a two-thirds majority vote of the Assembly of Heads of State and Government. Such amendments will come into force one year after submission.

MEMBER STATES OF THE ORGANIZATION

1. Algeria
2. Angola
3. Botswana
4. Burkina Faso
5. Burundi
6. Cameroon
7. Cape Verde
8. Central African Republic
9. Chad

10. Comoros
11. Congo
12. Djibouti
13. Egypt
14. Equatorial Guinea
15. Ethiopia
16. Gabon
17. The Gambia
18. Ghana
19. Guinea
20. Guinea-Bissau
21. Ivory Coast (Cote d'Ivoire)
22. Kenya
23. Lesotho
24. Liberia
25. Libya
26. Madagascar
27. Malawi
28. Mali
29. Mauritania
30. Mauritius
31. *Morocco
32. Mozambique
33. Niger
34. Nigeria
35. Rwanda
36. Sao Tome and principe
37. Senegal
38. Seychelles
39. Sierra Leone
40. Somalia
41. Sudan
42. The Sahrawi Arab Democratic Republic
43. Swaziland
44. Tanzania
45. Togo
46. Tunisia

47. Uganda
48. Zaire
49. Zambia
50. Zimbabwe

*Morocco withdrew from the OAU membership in November 1985 as a result of the admittance of the Sahrawi Arab Democratic Republic, otherwise known as Western Sahara, in February 1982. It claimed that two-thirds majority and not a simple majority was needed to admit a state whose existence was in question.

Nonetheless, the Moroccan authorities have signalled their interest to rejoin the OAU in 1989, after nearly four years of absence. A lot of people believe that Morocco lost the bid to host the World Soccer Championship competition in 1990 to the United States of American which is not known in the soccer field, because of its withdrawal from the OAU. The organization exercised indifference during the bidding process of the soccer championship games.

> *"Things fall apart: The centre cannot hold.*
> *Mere anarchy is loosed upon the world*
> *The blood-dimmed tide of innocence Is loosed and everywhere.*
> *The ceremony of innocence is drowned.*
> *The best lack all conviction, while the worst*
> *Are full of passionate intensity."*
>
> *Yeats Poem - The Second Coming*

* * *

AFRICA AND THE WORLD

"Africa was the mother of mankind," the place where Homo-sapiens first emerged, wrote Basil Davidson, in his Africa In History: Themes and Outlines. R. Oliver and J. O. Fage, in their "A Short History of Africa," published in 1962, concurred, but in a different style. They wrote that in the Stone Age, Africa was "not even relatively backward: it was in the lead."

In their "First, We Were Africans,"

Langston Hughes, Milton Meltzer, and C. Eric Lincoln, in their book, "A Pictorial History of Black Americans," wrote, "Africa is an ancient land. For thousands of years before history was reduced to writing, generations upon generations of black men were locked in an unremitting struggle with their environment in the determination that life should have meaning and purpose beyond mere survival. There are many 'Cradles of Civilization' in the ancient river valleys of the world, where because of a unique balance of ecological factors, survival-plus made possible the emergence of cultures. But increasingly the careful reading of nature's own records seems to show that Africa not only gave the world its earliest civilizations, she gave the world man. The evidence is there under the patterned layers of earth in the Olduvai Gorge in East Africa, preserved by the hot dry sands of the Sahara, and beneath the mud and silt of centuries in the valley of the Nile."

"Many geologists believe," wrote (now late) Prof. Stanlake Samkange of Harvard University in U.S.A., in his African Saga, written about three decades ago, "that about three hundred million years ago, Africa was united with other continents of the world in one vast landmass they have given the name Gondwanaland. Geologists hold this view because of the remarkable similarities in the geological record of different continents, as well as important biological links found among them . . . The importance of the Gondwanaland theory to students of history," he wrote, "lies in the suggestion it offers about how the ancestors of man and, indeed man himself, may have migrated from one area - Africa - to the rest of the world."

As recently as today, the above assertions still hold relevance. The Newsweek (U.S.A.) article of January 11, 1988, proclaimed that "Scientists claim to have found our common ancestor -- a woman who lived 200,000 years ago and left resilient genes that are carried by all mankind. The scientists' Eve-- subject of one of the most provocative anthropological theories in a decade-- was more likely a dark-haired, black-skinned woman, roaming a hot Savanna in search of food," said the paper. "She was as muscular as Martina Navratilova, may be stronger; she might have torn animals apart with her hands, although she probably preferred to use stone tools. She was not the only woman on earth, nor necessarily the most attractive or maternal. She was simply the most fruitful, if that is measured by success in propagating a certain set of genes. Hers seem to be in all humans living today: 5 billion blood relatives. She was, by one rough estimate, your 10,000th great-grandmother . . . Most evidence so far indicates that Eve lived in sub-Sahara Africa . . ."

"The most controversial implication of the geneticists work," the paper continued, "is that modern humans did not slowly and inexorably evolve in different parts of the world, as many anthropologists believed. The evolution from archaic to modern Homo sapiens seems to have occurred in only one place: Eve's family. Then, sometime between 90,000 and 180,000 years ago, a group of her progeny left their homeland endowed apparently with some special advantage over every tribe of early humans they encountered. As they fanned out, Eve's descendants replaced the locals, eventually settling the entire world.

"Some 'stone-and-bones' anthropologists accept this view of evolution," while some "think our common ancestor must have lived much farther in the past, at least a million years ago, because that was when humans first left Africa and began spreading out over the world, presumably evolving separately into the modern races . . ."

"Either way," said the paper, "it appeared that all these ancient humans traced their lineage back to Africa, because that was the only place with evidence of humans living more than a million years ago. Stone tools were invented there about 2 million years ago by an ancestor named Homo habilis (Handy man). Before him was Lucy, whose 3 million-year-old skeleton was unearthed in the Ethiopian desert in 1974."

How was this mysterious Eve discovered? To find her, Dr. Rebecca Cann first had to persuade 147 pregnant women to donate their babies' placentas to science. The placentas were the easiest way to get large samples of body tissue. Working with Prof. Allan Wilson and a biologist, Prof. Mark Stoneking, all of the University of California at Berkeley, Cann, formerly at Berkeley, but at this time at the University of Hawaii, selected women in America with ancestors from Africa, Europe, the Middle East and Asia. Her collaborators in New Guinea and Australia found aboriginal women there.

After their babies were born, the placentas were gathered and frozen. The tissues analysis began at Wilson's lab in Berkeley. The tissues were ground in a soup-up waring blender, spun in a centrifuge, mixed with a cell-breaking detergent, dyed fluorescent and spun in a centrifuge again. The result was a clear liquid containing pure DNA.

According to the report, scientists didn't learn that the Mitochondrion contained any genes until the 1960's. In the late 1970's, they discovered that Mitochondrial DNA was useful for tracing family trees because it is inheritable only from the mother.

The findings also showed that "there were not even tell-tale distinctions between races." "We're a young species, and there are really very few genetic differences among cultures," said Stoneking. "In terms of our Mitochondrial DNA, we're much more closely related than almost any other vertebrate or mammalian species. You find New Guineans whose DNA is closer to other Asians than other New Guineans," he said. DNA - deoxyribonucleic acid - is now an accepted technique, which can identify with great probability the genetic patterns from blood, semen or other body fluids.

In the study, many differences represent trivial changes. But what about the skin colour? Well, skin colour is said to be as a result of "minor adaptation to climate -- black in Africa for protection from the sun, white in Europe to absorb ultraviolet radiation that helps produce vitamine D. It takes only a few thousand years of evolution for skin colour to change. . ."

"At the moment," the study emphasized, "the evidence seems to favour an African Eve, because other genetic studies (of nuclear DNA) also point to an origin there and because that's where the earliest fossils of modern humans have been found."

How does this correlate with Hugh Trevor-Roper, Rigins Professor of History at Oxford University, England, who once said in his "The Rise of Christian Europe," that "Undergraduates seduced as always, by the changing breath of journalistic fashion, demand that they should be taught the history of black Africa. Perhaps, in the future there will be some African history to teach. But at present there is none, or very little: there is only the history of Europeans in Africa. The rest is darkness . . . And darkness is not subject for history. Please do not misunderstand me." He hurriedly added that "Men existed even in dark countries and dark centuries," but to study their history, he continued, would be to "amuse ourselves with the unrewarding gyrations of barbarious tribe in picturesque but irrelevant corners of the globe."

Professor Roper, if alive today, would be mystified to learn that Africa has eternally had immortal and undeniable history, and that utter feebleness, laziness and ignorance blind-folded his thinking faculty and imagination from delving into research and exploring such neglected rich African past.

This finding, with other unqualified studies and assertions of anthropologists, sociologists, paleographers, archaeologists, anatomists, musicologists, physiologists, and numismatists world-wide, dwarf the self-aggrandisement of the early European scholars of (Charles Robert) Darwinism, which suggested that the major races had each descended from different species of ape: Caucasians from chimpanzees, which is assumed to be the most intelligent non-human primates; Orientals from orangutans; and Negroes from gorillas, the biggest and darkest of all.

The emerged unquestionable evidence showing that the early man came from Africa, gives more credence to the epistemology that Jesus Christ was a black man. As Prof. Samkange wrote, "As a matter of fact, Eisler tells us that according to Josephus, a Jewish historian of the first century, Christ 'was a man of simple appearance, mature age, dark skin, short growth, three cubits, hunch-backed . . . with scanty hair . . . and with an under-developed beard."

Even prophet Isaiah, in Isaiah 53:2 said of the Messiah, "He hath no form or comeliness, and when we shall see him, there is no beauty that we shall desire him." And Numbers 12:1 tells us for certain that the respected Moses that helped the Israelis to cross the Red Sea on their way to the promised land, chose a black woman, an Ethiopian, to be his wife, bearing in mind that Moses was a Jew, and the Ethiopian, in Jewish terminology, a Gentile.

There is also the story of a black man who complained to Jesus Christ, according to biblical studies, that some white men were refusing him admission to a certain church because of his colour. Christ reportedly replied to him, "Don't I know it? I have been trying to enter that church myself all these years. They won't let me in." Even today, if Christ would come again as a black man, he most probably would be rejected because of some built-in stereotype against the pigmentation and etymology of a black man in most quarters. It is fair, however, to say that some blacks would reject him too, in part, because of some brain-washing and/or "brain-sterilization" inflicted on them by their former colonial, and in some areas, slave masters, or by mere ignorance, atheism, and geo-political schism in their midst. Besides, some Blacks do not even respect their fellow Blacks.

Perhaps that is why the Vatican City, the religious and political seat of the Catholic Church, does not believe that African Reverend Fathers can perform miracles through the God "thy God." Their skepticism probably emanates from the view that there has not been a "black" Pope.

The Right Rev. Millingo, the Catholic Archbishop of Lusaka, Zambia, reportedly heals the sick, casts demons, and what have you, among religious faithfuls, both Black and White people within his spiritual domain, with prayers. He had even performed that in Rome. But the Vatican thought that he was using Voodoo in his practice because his spiritual powers were "uncatholic." This merited a headline on NBC (USA) Network News of February 4, 1989, with Connie Chung, a Chinese American as the anchor.

How did Archbishop Millingo learn the usage of voodoo? At the Catholic Seminary School or as an Archbishop? Independent sources reported that he was subjected to some psychological and psychiatric evaluation and/or examination by the Vatican to see why he had such spiritual powers that even the Pope, the King of Kings of the Catholic clergies, did not have.

Does the doubt on this Holy Black African Right Rev. Father Millingo make mockery of the "Holy" Catholic Church? If any shadow of doubt can be cast on an Archbishop, what of when the Almighty carries His wishes through a mere Reverend Father, or a layman?

In Nigeria, particularly in the Eastern part, there is renewed hope in Christianity now because of one Rev. Father (name withheld). It is said that he can foretell through vision, heal the sick and lunatic, make one confess spiritually, tell one what one's real problem is, correctly predict if one has voodoo, etc. What is his weapon for this work? Prayer, independent sources affirm.

His blessed holy water is now in high demand in Nigeria. The faithfuls and believers travel hundreds of miles to his parish in a remote town (Elele) in River State, Nigeria for his Eucharist and holy water.

As a Catholic ordained Priest, he reportedly was not accepting gifts or cash for his God's work unless it was donated specifically to the church. African parishioners, unlike those of the United States of America, donate what is from their heart and not a mandatory 10% or certain percentage of their annual income.

Now there is a sticker with dove sign on it that people place on their car windshields. Any of those cars with the sticker or blessed by this Rev. Father, if stolen, is almost always returned untampered.

Is there any similarity between this Reverend Father and the Archbishop of Lusaka, Zambia, mentioned earlier? It seems that the more popular a priest is in the Catholic Church, the more threatened the Vatican feels. Perhaps that was why the Rev. Martin Luther bolted out from that Church, thus, the birth of protestantism today.

And perhaps, all these happenings, including those yet to happen, should be a forewarning that Christ is likely to come again as a Black person, even if it is debatable whether He was ever a Black man.

Now search your soul, and answer this question: How many of you are ready to accept him as the Messiah if he comes (again) as a Black man? That is a test of Christianity, if there is actually a true Christian in this materialistic and political world.

It is now well accepted that early civilization of man came from Africa. It was reported that when Napoleon invaded Egypt in 1798, his archaeologists and scientists found ancient monuments, well-preserved mummies, evidence of the beginning of science and art. (Egyptian Ramses The Great exhibits, mummies, and ancient arts were displayed in Dallas, Texas, USA from March 5, 1989 to August 19, 1989.) They came to realize that the origins of western civilization were much earlier than the Greeks or Romans. Though the population which Frenchmen found in the country was racially mixed, Napoleon's scientists came to the conclusion that ancient Egyptians were Negroid. It was equally noted, according to Sanders Hamitic Hypothesis, that one member of that expedition named Baron Denon, described the people as having "A broad and flat nose, very short, a large flattened mouth . . . thick lips, etc."

Sanders also cited that Constantin Volney, a famous French traveller who earlier had spent four years in Egypt and Syria, wrote in his abject disgust with slavery, "How are we astonished . . . when we reflect that to the race of Negroes, at present our slaves, and objects of our contempt, we owe our arts, sciences, and . . . when we recollect that, in the midst of these nations, who call themselves the friends of liberty and humanity, the most barbarous of slaveries is justified; and that it is even a problem whether the understanding of Negroes be of the same species with that of white men."

Again, wrote Hughes, Meltzer, and Lincoln: "Meaningful survival. That is the essence of civilization. That is the stuff of culture. The Africans survived; they learned to cope with the rivers and the forest, the lion, the leopard, and the crocodile; they learned the names and the characters of the gods. They flourished and built civilizations. Great civilizations.

"In Egypt, they labored to build the pyramids and the temples thousands of years before Europe developed a stable civilization. Black Pharaohs ruled Egypt for centuries and Black Queen Nefretete, one of the most beautiful women of all time, graced the Egyptian throne as the wife of Aahmes 1, to become cofounder of the great Eighteenth Dynasty."

Continued these history authorities, "The Greeks and the Romans knew of and wrote about the black peoples of Egypt and Ethiopia. Secular history and the Holy Scriptures of three great religions bear irrefutable testimony to the African influence on the development of Judaism, Christianity, and Islam. If Hagar had not borne a child for Abraham; if Ebedmelech had not rescued the Prophet Jeremiah from the dungeon; if the Queen of Sheba had not captured the admiration of Solomon; if Abdul Hasan Ali, black Sultan of Morocco, had not befriended Mohammed, the course of religious history would have been changed for countless millions of believers," they stressed.

Talking of civilization still, Egypt, an African country, employed decimal system, linear measure, keeping records of affairs; there was an institute for the study of astronomy at Heliopolis. This city was also the centre of the sun cult in which great emphasis was placed on determining the movement of the heavenly bodies. A calendar based on twelve months of thirty days, plus five scattered feast days, was introduced during the archaic period. By 2500 B.C., an even more accurate calendar had been developed.

In Amiri, Oru Local Government Area, Imo State, Nigeria, most people, especially staunch traditionalists, do not care about any other calendar but their own which recognizes their four market days, namely Orie, Afor, Nkwo, and Eke. This system applies to most Igbo land of former Eastern Region of Nigeria. Even those market days have certain prefix of Eke-nta, Eke-Ukwu, Orie-nta, Orie-Ukwu, etc., meaning grand or lighter market day of each of the four revolving days.

If a person dies, he cannot be buried on certain days. For instance, in Amiri, the dead cannot be buried on Orie or Oghu Festival day. The remains are either buried before or after Orie or Oghu day. To bury someone on any of those designated days is prohibited by the(ir) customs.

Through their system of market days, they figure out weeks, months and years. When this author was growing up, his venerated late grandmother, Ihesi Nwachukwu, did not know, nor did she care about any other system of calendar but theirs. It has endured for centuries. From their calendar, they figure out their festivities of the year, such as Oghu (pronounced as Owu), Okposi, etc., and the exact market days they would fall in.

It must be recalled that most of the seven wonders of the world came from Africa, among which was the Pyramid still in existence today in Egypt.

In addition to Egypt, Ethiopia helped in the civilization of the world. Wrote W. E. B. Dubois a quarter of a century ago, in his World and Africa, "In Ethiopia the sunrise of human culture took place, spreading down into the Nile Valley. Ethiopia, land of the Blacks, was the cradle of Egyptian civilization."

Wrote Ronald W. Davis in his Negro Contributions to the Explorations of the Globe, "Africans along this (Atlantic) Coast had been seeing foreign ships for centuries. In 1417 and again in 1422, Chinese ships had called on the east coast of Africa. So when the Portuguese came, Africans saw nothing to be excited about. Vasco da Gama was taken to Malindi where he engaged an African pilot, Ibn Madjid who piloted him to India. This seaman was the author of a set of instructions on navigating in the capricious Monsoon winds of the Indian Ocean, and he knew the Indian Ocean as the palm of his hand."

The Eastern Coast of Africa which Vasco da Gama came had long been "In direct contact with the Southern shores of Arabia, Southern Persia, Western India, and the islands of the Indonesian

archipelago for over two thousand years."
At this time, Europeans nursed none of
the ideas of racial superiority later to
be characteristic of them. Africans, on
their part, did not suffer from any
inferiority complex. Wrote Basil
Davidson on Black Mother, if anything,
Africans considered themselves superior,
as Father Cavazzi reported from the Congo
in 1687: "With nauseating presumption,
these nations think themselves, the
foremost men in the world, and nothing
will persuade them to the contrary. They
imagine that Africa is not only the
greatest part of the world, but also the
happiest and most agreeable. Similar
opinions are held by the king himself but
in a manner still more remarkable. For
he is persuaded that there is no monarch
in the world who is his equal or exceeds
him in power or the abundance of wealth."

Although this feeling still prevails
to date in most African nations, Chaka
Zulu, one of the early Kings in Southern
African Region, is a memorable example.
He was very sagacious.

It is noted that European observers
of Benin Empire -- now part of present
Nigeria in Bendel State -- in the 17th
century were impressed by the efficiency
of its government. Wrote John Barbot,
"The King might be considered just and
equitable, as desiring continually his
officers to administer justice exactly,
and to discharge their duties

conscientiously. . ." As quoted by Basil Davidson in Black Mother: The Years of the African Slave Trade, "He (the Benin King) seldom passes one day, without holding a cabinet council with his Chief Ministers, for dispatching of many affairs brought before him. . . appeals from inferior courts of judicature in all parts of the Kingdom, and audiences to strangers, or concerning the affairs of war and other emergencies."

As Dr. Kwame Nkrumah of Ghana wrote in his famous book, I Speak of Freedom, published in New York in 1961, "For the one thousand years that Ghana Empire existed, it spread over a wide expanse of territory in the Western Sudan. Its influence stretched across the Sudan from Lake Chad in the East to the Futa Jalon Mountains in the West and from the Southern fringes of the Sahara Desert in the North to the Bights of Benin and Biafra in the South. Thus the Ghana Empire was known to have covered what is now the greater part of West Africa-- namely, from Nigeria in the East to Senegambia in the West. While it existed, the Ghana Empire carried on extensive commercial relations with the outside world -- extending as far as Spain and Portugal. Gold, animal skins, ivory, kola-nuts, guns, honey, corn and cotton were among the articles that writers had most frequently named.

"It is reported," he continued,

"that Egyptians and Asiatic students attended the great and famous universities and other institutions of higher learning that flourished in Ghana during the medieval period to learn philosophy, mathematics, medicine and law."

Writing along the same line as Dr. Nkrumah, Hughes, Meltzer and Lincoln asserted that "A number of superior civilizations rose and fell in West Africa before the coming of the white man. Ancient Ghana was flourishing about the time of the Roman invasion of Britain, and did not begin to decline until the eleventh century. At the height of its glory, Ghana boasted a standing army of 20,000 men, their horses caparisoned in cloth made of gold. An honor guard, bearing golden shields and gold-mounted swords, with gold plaited into their hair, waited upon the King. The King's splendidly attired attendants were seconded by dogs of an excellent breed, wearing collars of gold and silver, who never left the King's seat."

Continued Hughes and his co-authors, "Ghana's splendor was succeeded by Mali, a small state whose history antedated that of Ghana by two hundred years, but which did not attain importance until the twelfth century when, through a series of conquests under Sundiata Keita, it became a great empire. By the fourteenth century it was described as rich, well-ordered state. Mali was a moslem state, and in 1324 its ruler, Mansa Musa, made a pilgrimage to Mecca. It was undoubtedly one of the most regal pilgrimages of all time, involving an entourage of 60,000 persons. There were 2,000 servants, 500 slaves (with gold staffs), and eighty camels laden with more than two tons of gold to be distributed among the poor . . ."

"Mali waxed and waned as civilizations do," they wrote, "and was in time eclipsed by the Kingdom of Songhay under Askia Mohammed Askia who came to power about the time Columbus was reporting his 'discovery' of America to Queen Isabella of Spain. Remarkably, Askia's Kingdom covered most of West Africa and was greater than all of the European states combined. Historians acclaim his rule as one of great plenty and absolute peace. Under Askia," these authors stressed, "Timbuktu became a thriving commercial cross-roads of 100,000 people, where the merchants from distant lands came in endless caravans to exchange their exotic center unrivaled at the time. To its famous University of Sankore came the ambitious youth from the Moslem world to study law and medicine. Medieval Europe sent its best scholars there to see the great libraries with manuscripts in Greek and Latin as well as in Arabic, and to consult with the learned mathematicians, astronomers, physicians, and jurists whose intellectual endeavo(u)rs were paid for out of the King's own treasury."

M. Perham and J. Simmons, in their book titled, African Discovery: Anthology of Exploration, first published in 1942, stated that, "The beautiful bronzes and ivories of Benin (in Nigeria) were discovered in 1897. The first of the magnificent bronzes of Ife (in Nigeria), the earliest of which dated from the 13th century and owe nothing to Europe, was not found until 1910 and the main collection did not come to light until 1938."

Dr. Basil Davidson, in his Old Africa Rediscovered, first published in 1959, stated that, "Europeans stumbled on the great stone remains of Zimbabwe in 1868 . . . Radio Carbon tests have yielded dates between the 5th and 15th centuries A. D. and combined with other archaeological evidence leave no serious doubt that they were an African creation."

It is very ironical that Africa, which was the mother of man, and where the cradle of civilization began, is ranking almost last among all the continents of the world today. It is now regarded as a third world. Even Ethiopia, never colonized, is surviving at the mercy of the generous contribution of the world (remember "We are the world" record music by U. S. artists), to its famine stricken victims. The major cause of the famine though, as many people knew, was drought -- an act of God.

Egypt, which once housed and enslaved Israelis, and where one of the seven wonders of the world -- pyramid-- is still visible, succumbed to Israeli military might in 1967, and perhaps, to the present. This must not be unconnected with the signing of the peace accord, known as Camp David Accord in U. S. during the tenure of peace loving President Jimmy Carter, with Israel in March 1979. The major price paid for this gesture by Egypt was her ostracism by other Arab world which did not want the existence of Israel. Technological advancement, relative to the now developed world, seems to sound foreign to the present Egyptian generation.

Wrote Professor Stanlake Samkange in his Wars of Resistance to European Rule, "The journeys (of the Europeans to Africa) had another merit: They portrayed Africa as a virgin land for the planting of christianity. So, European missionaries went to Africa to preach the gospel. They wore out soles saving souls; but too often found themselves the agents of life through death, peace through war, accord through discord, education through westernization, civilization through dehumanization, and construction through destruction. For they were soon persuaded that only

through waging ruthless war of conquest
. . . could peace reign in Africa. Only
through discord, inherent in the
injection of christianity and the
rejection of traditional African ideas of
God, could accord be achieved. Only by
keeping Africans ignorant of the good in
their culture and the greatness in their
history, by teaching them Western values
and the superiority of Europeans, could
they be educated. Only through the
abandonment of a native culture based on
humanistic, family and tribal ties,
responsibilities and sanctions, and the
imposition of a dehumanizing,
individualistic, and materialistic one,
could Africans be civilized. Only
through the total destruction of African
ideas, values, and mores could new Africa
be built."

The so-called individualism and
materialism are among the reasons most
African nations are in disarray today.
This inevitably led to bribery and
corruption, embezzlement, forgery,
dishonesty, armed robbery and other
felonious crimes. Greediness continued
to cloud serenity and justice.

Even nuclear, radio-active, toxic
and other industrial wastes from the
developed world are now finding their way
into African soil for burial.
Unbeknownst to Major-General Ike
Nwachukwu, the Nigerian External Affairs
Minister, as he was addressing the United

Nations General Assembly in June 1988 to make "a clear and unequivocal statement on the callous and insensitive attempts" at dumping waste in Africa, the toxic waste from Italy was already laying on the soil of his beloved country. Some unscrupulous Nigerians in collaboration with some Italians residing in Nigeria, such as Gianfranco Raffaelli, formed a "shell" corporation called Iruekpen Construction Company (ICC), to import chemicals from Italy for their work. That "chemical" was toxic waste.

Through the connivance of the Nigerian Ports Authority agents, Custom Personnel and Health officials, the "imported chemicals" passed without inspection at Koko Port in Bendel State of Nigeria where fewer experts were normally posted. The over 1,000 crates and sacks containing the wastes were actually moved into the Koko town since September 21, 1987 without notice. It was twelve Nigerian students studying in Italy, namely Francis Kolawole Eludini, David Olusegun, Peter Ogordi, Udo Enwereuzor, B. Nade, Etu Umo, Thaddaeus Onuchukwu, Johnson Niyi Laniyonu, Babatunde Fadeyi, Ihekwoaba A. Chimezie, Oduneye Bamidele, and Samuel Oduche, that alerted the bewildered and stunned government through the respected and aggressive Nigerian Press with overwhelming evidence.

The most disappointing part of this

was that not only was the Italian Ambassador to Nigeria aware of this, Raffaelli who orchestrated this nightmare bribed himself out of Nigeria through the Immigration point at Murtala Muhammed International Airport, Lagos, without his passport. He reportedly bribed himself out of the country with 1,700.00 Naira after his passport was seized by the authorities.

The reason the Nigerian case was unique was that the high echelon of the government did not sanction it like that of Guinea, Djibouti, Benin Republic, Venezuela in Latin America, Rumania in Eastern Europe, Lebanon in the Middle East, etc. As Major-General Ike Nwachukwu muttered after he was made aware of this shortly after his speech in New York in June 1988, "Someone has hit us below the belt." The Nigerian government acted promptly. It seized Italian ships. To wade off a diplomatic storm with Nigeria, Italy agreed to pay for the cost of the evacuation of the waste it helped to dump illegally.

Two of the three ships used to send back the waste to Italy, or who knows where now in Europe, were Karin B and The Deep Sea Carrier, all of Italy. The last shipment back to Italy was about August 11, 1988. What a bold move by Nigeria. Said President Babangida of Nigeria, "No government, no matter the financial inducement, has the right to mortgage the destiny of future generations of African children."

Because of money, some Africans were selling their birthright, and ultimately sowing the seeds of death. Money for death? Matthew Kerekou of Benin Republic reportedly attempted to rescind his contract of dumping toxic waste in his country, but it was too late, because part of the advance payment to his government had been used. After the revelation, his regime became shaky. He allegedly has about a dozen houses overseas and millions of dollars in foreign banks. Now one can imagine why Africa is falling apart, as things are no longer at ease.

In African Culture, the elders usually hand the young some unwritten wisdom. Where such youngster bluffs or puffs the knowledge or idea, perhaps due to the so-called westernization, the wisdom becomes lost. Apparently he would have nothing very unique and pertinent from his past "mentors" to hand down to his own children, and the cycle, to the disadvantage of the society, may continue.

The emergence of slave trade in Africa was one of the major factors Africa fell to colonization, thus, her scramble and partition. Wrote Dr. Samkange, "Because Africa emerged from the slave trade depopulated and divided, its people weak and suspicious of one another, it fell easy prey to machination, colonization schemes, and armies of Europeans." This shows that a house (that is) divided cannot stand.

To some western countries where international historical ignorance and subterfuge of false racial superiority prevail over geographical and authentic historical knowledge and curiosity, exacerbated by their "political" media, either by commission, omission, or design, the insensitivity of seeing Africans not from their cultural relativism and adopted mores, but on their (west) own exaggerated and self-exalted cultural standard, shamelessly continue unabated.

The United States of America which tried centuries ago to dehumanize the descendants of the Black adventurers and indentured servants with the full cooperation of the British, are the most culprit of this ugly and reprehensible behaviour. Their media, mostly owned, anchored, analysed and reported by the "whites" who believe in the status quo of the past, aid and abet the dichotomous and anachronistic situation. But with hope, Africa will rise again. On its second coming, it must have learned a lesson.

* * *

FOREIGN MEDIA AND AFRICA

The Western media rarely portray Africa in a glamorous light. It always puts her in a degrading falsehood. In the United States of America where people learn almost everything through the television, radio and newspaper, Africa is always shown as a rag-tag continent. It is even hardly shown as a continent with nearly fifty-two sovereign nations. Probably because some African countries suppress information, they try to coin their own exaggerated "news". Even if accurate information is given, it is certain to be distorted anyway, to make news to the west as usual.

During this author's freshman year at Alabama A & M University, his History (101) Professor one day decided to quiz the students on their knowledge of Africa. She asked a multiple choice question thus: Africa is (A) A country; (B) County; (C) Continent; or (D) City. Eighty percent of the class failed this quiz. This shows one how America prepares or teaches her citizens the world history.

This University happens to be among the very few that offer World History as a mandatory course to all students instead of just American History. In most American universities, American History is a core course. World History is usually viewed as irrelevant unless one is a history major. Then, imagine how much world history experience the(ir) secondary school students and graduates would have. This is the reason most of them who don't study beyond their school syllabus believe that America is the world, instead of a tiny fraction of the earth, her wealth, power and great influence notwithstanding.

Said Prof. William Holmes of the University of North Texas, formerly North Texas State University, according to the Dallas Morning News of July 29, 1988, about Americans' lack of world knowledge: "To us professors, it is no surprise. We have known for a long time that Americans are generally ignorant about the world . . ."

In a release of a report on the dismal state of Americans' knowledge about the globe by the (American) National Geographic Society, its president, Gilbert M. Grosvenor, an American, said of his people, "They are lost. They haven't the faintest idea where they were . . ." Among Americans tested, 14% could not pick out the United States on a world map. In a survey among

18 to 24-year-olds which included Sweden, West Germany, Japan, Canada, Italy, France, United Kingdom, Mexico, and the United States, the result was in that order. The United States finished dead last.

No American medium has taken the courage to show anything good, optimistic, or emulous about Africa. When there is a successful breakthrough in anything in Africa, it is largely ignored. When there is schism or any sort of disaster, even if it is an act of God, it is usually blown out of proportion as the American Broadcasting Corporation (ABC), among other network news, showed on August 9, 1988 (5:30 p.m. news, Central Standard Time), the disastrous torrential rain in Sudan, in North East Africa. As the ABC anchorman, a Canadian born Peter Jennings mentioned the Sudanese capital, Khartoum, the network's cameraman showed some slums in the countryside being swept by the torrential rain; thus, projecting the image as if that was the capital.

On September 27, 1988 when NBC -- a U.S. television network that bought the exclusive rights to show the Seoul, South Korea 1988 24th Olympiad games in U.S. -- was profiling Kenya, the only thing it showed was wild life animals. Not even a single decent human being or good inhabitable building was shown. Not even the track athletic star that won a gold medal for Kenya a day earlier was shown. We probably have to ask Connie Chung who anchored it, why?

Kenya ended up bagging 5 golds, 2 silver, and 2 bronze medals during that Olympic. The U.S. network did not have the courtesy to show when the national anthem of Kenya was played in honour of the championship it won meritoriously. The reason behind all these is to erroneously show that it is the way Africa is, or ought to be.

Take the case of "Tarzan" movies shown in American television. It is the worst blatant depiction of African life. Still, a lot of Americans and other civilized world do not realize that it is a fake television programme which some unscrupulous white men use to degrade Black Africans in particular, and black men in general. It beats one hollow to see such erroneous depiction of jungle livelihood on innocent, rational, educated and civilized Africans. Why such films are shot still baffles man. And why such caricatural, demagogical and insulting film is aired is another question.

That underscores why some Americans think (some still do) that Africans live on the tops of trees. When this author showed some pictures of some tourist attractions, where he lived and worked in his country, his American friends were stunned as opposed to what they saw on television news and Tarzan. Even when Pope John Paul II visited Nigeria in early 1983, at an open field mass conducted at Onitsha, Anambra State, the Dallas daily newspaper carried on the front page a picture of a boy who climbed a nearby flower tree to have a glimpse of the Pope. This again portrayed the stereotype in more ways than writing.

There was one ridiculous incident that happened in Dallas, Texas fairly recently. There was one black lady with children who was planning an adventurous vacation to one African nation. When she made her plan known to the family, one of her children started fuming; this later converted into crying with a spark of a joke. A reasonable person would think that the child was fuming because he would miss the mother during the period of her absence. Hell no.

The boy revealed that he was saddened, because the mother might fall for those "hungry Africans" he usually saw on the television, and might be tempted to bring them home. Now one can understand the evil of the American unspoken cold war against Africans, and perhaps all Black race through television propaganda. Thus, American kids believe that all Africans are destitute. They even forget that in the midst of American richness and flamboyancy, there are some destitute families, as well as homeless.

Perhaps someone needs to take them to downtown Houston, Los Angeles, Dallas, New York, Chicago, Detroit, Birmingham (Alabama), Baltimore, Philadelphia, Boston, Jersey City, Minneapolis, St. Paul, to mention just a few big cities in U. S. All these even happen with the government liberalism on welfare hand out to these destitute families. Then, what would life be like without any government assistantship to these poor poeple in the U. S., colour of the skin notwithstanding.

This author's wife was surprised when a small Black American girl who recognized her as an African at the apartments (they lived in the same apartment houses or complex) swimming pool, told her that she was lucky to have survived in Africa, where, according to her, everybody was hungry. Victoria's attempt to educate this small girl who had made up her mind about Africa, failed. Perhaps the only way she would change her mind or moderate her thought is either visiting some African countries, or getting a positive picture about Africa from the American television. Even today, some adults still ask if one drove from Africa to the U. S. A., or came by ship. Saying that plane lands in any African country sounds strange to many. Some of them have their mind chained to the fact that earlier arrivals to U. S., either as indentured servants or slaves, came by ship or boats.

Thanks to programmes like Children's International Summer Village which sponsor children from one country to another each summer year to see the real geography or witness history. About 50 children and 15 camp leaders visited Nigeria in the summer of 1988. The eleven-year olds who participated came from Netherlands, Sweden, Luxembourg, Norway, U.S.A., Japan, Portugal, Sierra Leone, and, of course, Nigeria (the host).

Entertained by students and professors from the school of Theatre Arts of the University of Ibadan, at the International School, Ibadan, Nigeria, the children had a glimpse of real African theatrical music and culture. Arthur Freeman, a black American, led the American delegation. At the end of their 4-week stay which ended about August 14, 1988, the children who had watched Tarzan movies, denounced that programme. From their experiences, they came to believe that some foreign media had not been fair to Africans, and such deceitful movies about Africa like Tarzan, which shows Africa as a jungle, should not be allowed to air. The Childrens' International Summer Village, founded by Doris Allen, a psychologist at the University of Cincinnati, Ohio, U.S.A. in 1952 was developed to foster understanding among the world's children. The idea was borne out of the views that the two world wars resulted from lack of good communication/understanding among nations, as well as complexities and dynamics of human nature.

Some journalists have started to ask themselves some questions. Thanks to Ted Koppel of ABC News who featured the lack of American network's coverage of Africa on his Night Line programme of Tuesday, August 30, 1988.

Featuring guests like Lawrence Grossman, former President of National Broadcasting Corporation (NBC), Alexander Cockburn, a columnist with "The Nation," and Organization of African Unity (OAU) Ambassador Youssoufou, they talked various reasons why Africa is not covered in the news unless there are some disastrous events. Even disastrous events are selective in coverage. The pogrom of the Hutu tribe in Burundi by the minority Hutsi tribe who controlled the armed forces and government was peripherally mentioned. During the clash, an estimated 40,000 people were reportedly killed, thousands injured, and about 120,000 people fled to the neighbouring Rwanda.

But in contrast, the American news network fully covered the West Germany Air Force show mid-air crash that claimed about 45 lives. Perhaps the American network news organizations' logical reason was that, Burundi, with a population of about 5 million was not well known. Well known or not, who would educate the American public?

It was understood during such rare Night Line programme, that the American network news companies don't care much about Africa any way. According to Grossman, money to send journalists to Africa was not the problem; the problem was that the interest (in Africa) was not there, and that a lot of people do not know much about Africa. Most American news organizations have journalists stationed only in South Africa which had some whites in it. Other African countries are covered from whatever sketchy news they can fetch from either the satellite or through the word of mouth.

Ambassador Youssoufou was quick to point out, following Ted Koppel's prodding questions, although diplomatically, that American network's racism has a lot to do with it. Mr. Cockburn who was also an author, concurred, but pointed out that the (American) Administration (government) most of the time set an agenda on what the media usually focus on. American media, although not spoon-fed on what to say by the U. S. government, turn attention mostly where the government focuses. They rarely out of their own volition, unlike the Nigerian private owned printing media, take up issues on their own. (Nigerian television network, owned by the government, is a different saga.) Cockburn added that during the treacherous era of Samoza regime in Nicaragua, nothing was said about it. But now that Daniel Ortega is leaning towards communism, and the American government of Ronald Reagan sees it as a threat to American security, focus promptly shifted. Other dictators in Latin and Central America are left alone as long as they are U.S. cronies.

It was also alleged during the programme that American media, with all their freedom of the press, act for entertainment and not for finding and giving information or knowledge. Ambassador Youssoufou equally pointed out that when drought ravaged and barrened some African land a few years ago, it was blown out of proportion. Now that there is rain and the likelihood of abundant harvest, nothing is said about it in the electronic media other than disastrous effects.

He quickly mentioned that even in South Africa, when bombs explode in Johannesburg and kill or injure one or two whites and also kill seven blacks, those of whites are emphasized. Those of seven blacks killed are neglected. Again, racism effect in slanting and/or sliding reports.

It is substantially true that the

American media follow their government's move. As Harry Belafonte once insisted, if America wants to stop apartheid today in South Africa, it will do it in a matter of weeks, if not days.

Even when there is a smooth transition of power, such as the one that took place in Dar es Salaam, Tanzania in November 1985 when the Hon. Dr. Julius Nyerere voluntarily relinquished his power to Ali Hassan Mwinyi, President of the semi-autonomous island of Zanzibar, it was ignored by the major newspapers and television network in the United States of America in particular, and other developed world in general. Should it have been a coup d'etat, it could have been fully reported, and perhaps fully monitored to epitomize some African ineptitude.

One of the newspapers in Texas (USA), whose recognition of the Tanzanian episode was commendable though, was Dallas Times Herald. In its editorial of November 8, 1985 titled "End of an Era in Tanzania," it stated that, "In a quiet, dignified ceremony in Dar es Salaam this week, Julius K Nyerere -- Tanzania's revolutionary leader, founding father and President -- relinquished the reins of power he has held since he led his country to independence from British colonial rule in 1961. It was a milestone not only for his young, troubled nation, but for the entire

African continent.

"Mr. Nyerere is the last of the young visionaries who led successful struggles for freedom in AFrica in the years after World War II, culminating in the termination of the British, French, and Portuguese colonial empires there. And true to his image as a statesman and man of principle, he was the only one to leave office voluntarily -- relinquishing his hold on the presidency to give new ideas a chance to grow.

"And that is necessary. Under Mr. Nyerere, Tanzania has remained politically stable during the decades of social and economic upheaval; and it has attained a literacy rate of 85% -- the highest on the continent and far above that of even these United States.

"Mr. Nyerere has been called the 'conscience of Africa' for his opposition to oppression: Tanzania provides a haven for South African expatriates (fighting apartheid), and Tanzanian troops drove the despotic Idi Amin from power in Uganda in 1979.

"But Mr. Nyerere concedes that his socialistic policies have failed to provide a sound economic base for his nation of 20 million: Tanzania remains one of the world's poorest countries. But to his credit, the government has been virtually corruption free during his

24-year reign.

"Mr. Nyerere recognizes that it is time for a change in policies, and he has turned over the helm to Ali Hassan Mwinyi, a former Ambassador to Egypt and President of the semi-autonomous Island of Zanzibar. We salute Mr. Nyerere for the courage and leadership he has shown and his selfless decision to step aside for a new order. And we wish the best to his successor, Mr. Mwinyi, who has a class act to follow and a tough road ahead."

As of 1988, the literacy rate in Tanzania has risen to about 90.4%. They target 97% literacy rate by the turn of the century. What a remarkable goal and achievement for a country with a population of about 23 million by mid-1988.

This kind of unbiased editorial to an African is an exception to American journalism and not the rule. Dallas Times Herald has tried in the past (as we cannot predict what its future editorial stance would be) to be objective and fair in international and domestic affairs. Due to this progressive effort, some self-proclaimed conservatives tag it a "liberal" newspaper. In fact, this newspaper, in February 1986, carried some excerpts of Winnie Nomzamo Mandela's autobiography titled, "Part of My Soul Went With Him." Thrilled by the excerpts, I wrote to the editor on March 3, 1986 as follows:

"I enjoyed the five consecutive excerpts of Winnie Mandela's autobiography, 'Part of My Soul Went With Him' that appeared on your newspaper, the 'Living' section, from February 9-13, 1986. In fact, as I read it, I reflected Correta Scott King, the widow of the late Rev. (Dr.) Martin Luther King, Jr.

"There is no doubt on my mind that part of my soul is with their struggle for equality and justice. It has been proven that such people who sacrifice their life and mundane comfort for the freedom of their people and humanity always have their place in history. The late Rev. (Dr.) Martin Luther King, Jr., is the latest example. Third Monday in January every year is now a federal holiday in U.S.A. in honour of this civil rights leader who fell to the bullet of an assassin (James Earl Ray) at Memphis, Tennessee's Lorraine Motel on April 8, 1968.

"We pray for the success of their struggle and overdue freedom from the white minority government in South Africa."

Some American television network and magazines in some cases treat Africa as a detached continent. After all, as stated earlier, it was the mother of mankind.

The Time Magazine (USA), on its November 4, 1985 issue displayed photographs of what it called "Global Family Album." In the so-called Global Album, there was no African Head of State. This conspicuous omission forced me to write to the Editor as follows:

"The photographs you displayed on pages 18-19 of your November 4, 1985 issue are a mockery of the 'Global Family Album.' The so-called portraits did not reflect global characteristics.

"I searched in vain to see any of the African Heads of State that attended the 40th Anniversary of the United Nations Organization existence. For you to write off a continent like Africa in your self-designated 'Global Family' of the United Nations is idiotic, arrogant, and ironical to say the least.

"I have abandoned any respect I might have had for the Time Magazine because of this bigoted portrayal. And as such, I will not renew my subscription when the current one expires, until the Time recognizes that the 'Globe' is made up of seven continents with various races."

The Time's (public relations') candid response to the matter from their editorial offices, saved them further embarrassment, and it is hereby evidenced by the reproduction of the letter.

TIME
THE WEEKLY NEWSMAGAZINE

TIME & LIFE BUILDING
ROCKEFELLER CENTER
NEW YORK 10020

ISABEL KOURI
EDITORIAL OFFICES

November 25, 1985

Dear Mr. Nwachukwu:

We are sorry you were offended by the fact that no African leader was included in "A Global Family Album." This was not a reflection of any negative attitudes toward Africa or Africans but simply a problem of space. Most of the leaders pictured were from major world powers or countries whose affairs (Nicaragua, for example) are currently front and center in public discussion. We wish it had been possible to print the photograph of every statesman who was courteous enough to pose for our photographer, and we can understand your disappointment that we did not do so. Thank you very much for your letter and the frankness of your criticism. The letter was circulated among several editors for their consideration. We value your interest.

Sincerely,

Isabel Kouri

Mr. Richard O. Nwachukwu

When "60 Minutes," a powerful Columbia Broadcasting Service (CBS) Television Network programme showed Nigeria on Sunday, December 4, 1983, it completely put her in a grave false light. With tendentious reporting and incomprehensible attitude, the most ugly part of Nigeria was shown. There was nothing wrong in showing the filthy part of Lagos, the "present" capital -- the "future" capital (from 1990) shall be Abuja -- but it would have augurred well, and objective too, to dilute those ugly sceneries with the achievements or some down-to-earth architectural masterpieces of the capital, state or the country. It was like coming to the United States to take pictures of the ghettos and/or those areas in Mississippi and Alabama states where pit toilet is still in use, irrespective of all the technological advancement of the country. Or, to bring it closer home, it is like coming to Dallas to take photographs of typical South and West Dallas areas without any picture of downtown or North Dallas.

Objectivity is very crucial in international reporting, because a picture portrays a thousand words. Even the former U.S. Ambassador to Nigeria protested and condemned that biased reporting.

Although the objective of the 60 Minutes programme was to expose the country which at the time was perhaps the most expensive nation in the world, showing the affluent areas too, and why they were relatively expensive was deliberately skewed and obscured in the report. Then, 27 days later, the military overthrew the legitimate, though corrupt, government.

The paradox of television sound bites was succinctly put by Jennifer Hammond of Presque Isle, Maine (U.S.A.), as written in the Newsweek issue of December 5, 1988. Said she, ". . . But even as television connects us with people and places we would never otherwise encounter, it separates us from reality by teaching us to see the world as fast-paced, easy-to-digest sound bites without any substance. Man cannot live by sound bites alone: there's a real world out there beyond the cameras, and we're fast losing touch with it as we barricade ourselves behind the screen." And there is no doubt that most reporters barricade their prejudice behind the screen too.

That is how the Western press treat Africa: with innuendo. Any African invention or award based on meritocracy is renegaded. Credit is hardly given to them by the so-called Western press. They try not to elevate and motivate the spirit of the Black man in their midst. After all, who owns the press? Who controls the press? Who determines what goes into the press and what constitutes news?

LAGOS, NIGERIA

As it is said, one who pays for the piper, dictates the tune. Is it the way it ought to be all the time? Save your breath. Things are constantly changing, and it will continue to change for the benediction of the neglected. As such, one whose kernels are cracked by the benevolent spirit, as Professor Chinua Achebe would like to infer from Igbo aphorism, should not forget to be humble.

The way the West perceives Africa in particular and Black man in general flabbergasts one. When an epidemic erupts even in their respective countries, they start to eye a Black man as the carrier or for the answer.

When Acquired Immunodeficiency Syndrome (AIDs) erupted in the United States of America in the early 1980s, the press and the so-called medical experts dichotomously ignored the homosexuals and I.V. drug users who brought the disease in the first place, and carried their epidemiological studies to some African countries, including the study of wild monkeys in Africa for pathological answers. At the height of the paranoia, they linked innocent Haitians as high risk, simply because Haiti was a black nation. Haiti was later exonerated and subsequently removed as "high risk." But by then the damage to the nation's reputation had been done already. AIDS is caused by Human Immunodeficiency Virus

(HIV).

As a matter of fact, AIDS is believed to have come about mostly from (white) homosexuals who usually had anal sex, otherwise known as sodomy. According to a message from the United States of America Surgeon General, mailed to almost every household in the U.S. in June 1988, signed by C. Everett Koop, M.D., Sc.D., titled "Understanding AIDS," "The male homosexual population was the first in this country (USA) to feel the effects of the (AIDS) disease." But he warned that "In spite of what you may have heard, the number of heterosexual cases is growing. People who have died of AIDS in the U.S. have been male and female, rich and poor, White, Black, Hispanic, Asian and American Indian."

Those who are bi-sexual -- that is partly homosexual or lesbian and partly heterosexual -- help spread the deadly epidemic faster to other innocent heterosexuals. Drug addicts who use common "shooting" needles for cocaine, crack, etc., also act as the agents for the cross-pollination. Some innocent victims, such as pregnant women, hemophiliacs, etc., through early medical ignorance, got the disease through blood transfusion.

Some of the insignificant cases found in a few African countries are believed to have been as a result of exosmosis through foreign servicemen and army personnel stationed there. They transmitted the virus to the whores and some innocent girls, who in turn transmitted it to their male counterparts. The so-called medical experts who visited some Central African countries happened to be from the West, particularly France, Britain, and the United States of America.

People, irrespective of their professional etiquette, try to skew and exaggerate facts to satisfy their innate racial bias. That, in most African opinion, was what the self-dubbed British, French, and American experts have done. If they were experts as claimed, they could have invented a cure for AIDS long before now.

Apparently these were what was lurking in the mind of the newly appointed Health Minister of Zimbabwe that forced him to change the rule on how AIDS is reported in his country. Army Brigadier Felix Muchemwa, a medical doctor, after being appointed in January 1988, ordered that before anyone could be told that he has AIDS, two tests, one of them called the Western blot test, must be performed. Said he, "For me to know the enemy and attack him, I must have good intelligence. I want a scientific basis before I tell someone he has a disease."

This is one of the best patriotic moves I have ever seen any African public official boldly assert. He told the so-called Western experts that if there is any AIDS in Zimbabwe, it is Zimbabwe's business, and that he wouldn't have the country used in a "racist campaign" to malign Africa.

Said David Wilson, a University of Zimbabwe psychologist who studies attitudes about AIDS: "There are two perspectives -- the Western perspective that Africa is blocking AIDS information . . . But I think the other side has to be emphasized, and that is the incredible damage that the initial evidence linking AIDS to Africa without sufficient basis did. People do see racism in that. And they may be right."

According to the Dallas Times Herald of July 5, 1988, "Homosexuality and intravenous drug abuse, associated with AIDS in the United States and Europe, are almost nonexistent here (Zimbabwe)." Still, these Africans are dogged with the accusation of withholding information. The West has started to mistake malnutrition that is rampant in some poor African countries to symptoms of AIDS. This short-sightedness is dangerous and humiliating. But meanwhile, hat has to be doffed to Brig. (Dr.) Muchemwa for being sensitive to the Western bigotry and the resultant effect to the African image, egotism and welfare.

History has shown that most venereal diseases came from Europe or the West. In 1494, wrote J. A. Rogers, "syphilis was discovered in Europe when there was great epidemic of it, two years before the discovery of the New World."

Who actually knows where the AIDS originated from. One thing that is known for certain is that homosexuals in America and some drug users that share needle, first reported the cases of AIDS that were ever known. That obviously implies that AIDS originated, most probably from America and/or Europe. Its appearance in Africa came from both their servicemen in Africa, and perhaps from sabotage. Nothing is impossible for the American CIA and their so-called experts to do. For example, according to Associated Press release, as reported by the Dallas Times Herald of Thursday, October 6, 1988, "The (U.S.) government has tentatively settled a lawsuit that charged the CIA used nine Canadians as guinea pigs in mind-control research that included doses of LSD, lawyers said Wednesday (October 5, 1988)."

" . . . Neither side would discuss the proposed settlement, which still needs final approval by top Justice Department officials. But sources said CIA agreed to pay a total of $750,000.00.

"The $9 million lawsuit claimed that

CIA-financed research into mind-control left permanent psychological or emotional damage on the nine patients who underwent treatment in the late 1950s at Allan Memorial Institute of McGill University in Montreal.

"The research conducted by the institute's director, the late Dr. Ewen Cameron, included a week-long sleep induced by drugs, doses of LSD and unusually intense electroshock therapy. The treatments also included sensory deprivation and what Cameron called 'psychic driving' -- the repeated playing of recorded messages into a patient's ears for 16 hours . . ."

It was in 1953 that the CIA began researching the effects of LSD and other mind-altering substances.

Now, how do we know that in the 1980s the CIA did not use Africans to test if AIDS virus can cause immune deficiency in them, perhaps through the use of drugs or transfusion of blood?

Only God will ever know this, unless He forces any of the agents to confess. Even if it happens, American media might not pursue it to its logical conclusion. The confessor might be regarded as a crazy man, assuming he is allowed to live his life.

Some African practices, including

native medicine, may be archaic, but they have survived millions of years with them. Nonetheless, they can only take what is good from the western culture and forsake the odious ones. After all, no particular system of anything is absolutely flawless.

Africans could have improved to the level of enviousness long time ago, but the developed countries have continued to undermine their efforts. They kill or instigate the killing of their able and patriotic leaders through their secret agents or hired natives. If the secret work of the American Central Intelligence Agency (CIA), Soviet K.G.B., (Komitet Gosudarstvennoi Bezopasnosti; that is, Committee for State Security) or the British Intelligence is made public, Americans, like others, would be surprised, baffled, and ultimately despise them. But that is the world.

Do you know that a black man was the first person on earth ever to reach the North Pole on April 6, 1909? Well, at long last, a due recognition was accorded him, although posthumously.

According to the Associated Press (in U.S.A.), as reported in the Dallas Morning News of Thursday, April 7, 1988, "The Black Codiscoverer of the North Pole received what one supporter called 'long overdue recognition' as his remains were reinterred with full military hono(u)rs

Wednesday (April 6, 1988) at Arlington National Cemetery" in the State of Virginia.

"Matthew Alexander Henson was the first to reach the North Pole and planted the American flag there 79 years ago Wednesday during a trek with Adm. Robert E. Peary and four Eskimos," the report continued. "Peary was buried at Arlington in 1920 and a huge monument to him was erected beside his grave. Henson, however, was buried in 1955 in a shared grave at Woodlawn Cemetery in New York because his wife could not afford a separate grave site."

According to Dr. S. Allen Counter, a Harvard Professor who successfully petitioned President Ronald Reagan to allow Henson's reinterment at Arlington Cemetery, "He was denied proper recognition because of racial attitudes of his time." Even Henson's American niece, Olive Henson Fulton recounted her own ordeal. When she was a school girl, she was punished by her teacher for insisting that a Black man, her relative, had helped discover the North Pole. Said her at the joyous occasion, " . . . Today I no longer quietly tell my friends and co-workers of the achievements of my uncle."

Before this recognition, however, American History had it that Adm. Robert E. Peary discovered the North Pole. Now, the history will be rewritten. And many more shall be rewritten too. Henson's grave epitaph (he was 88 years at his death) which was from his quotes, read, "The lure of the Arctic is tugging at my heart. To me the trail is calling! The old trail -- The trail that is always new."

Now, there are notes, according to the Washington Post of Wednesday, October 12, 1988, which indicated that Adm. Robert Peary knew he never reached the Pole.

Said the paper, "Long-suppressed navigational notes by Robert Peary, regarded by most historians as the first person to reach the North Pole (until recently), indicate that Peary knew he had come no closer than 121 miles to attaining his goal but claimed he had made it anyway.

"The notes, deciphered by Dennis Rawlins, a Baltimore astronomer and historian, could lay to rest one of the greatest geographical controversies of the 20th century . . .

"The new evidence indicates that Peary knew exactly how far he was and that the remaining distance was too much to cover when supplies were running low and warming weather threatened to make the floating ice too dangerous. It also shows Peary's claim, popularly described as 'discovering' the North Pole, to have been a hoax."

According to Rawlins, "Peary himself took steps to insure that the truth would survive."

The evidence consists of notes that Peary appears to have written while at his northernmost point during the 1909 expedition -- a slip of paper containing his sextant readings and other calculations he made to determine his position. He kept the documents secret. Several years after his death, it was placed with his other papers, in the National Archives.

There, according to the Washington Post, the papers were kept from public scrutiny until Peary's descendant unsealed the files in 1984.

Rawlins emphasized that from the data on the suppressed document, he calculated that Peary gave up his quest for the Pole at a point within two nautical miles of 88 degrees 15' north latitude and 14 degrees west longitude, assuming his watch was accurate.

At long last, the truth is gradually emerging. At long last, Matthew Alexander Henson, a black man, is now recognized as the first person to reach the North Pole and planted the American flag there on April 6, 1909. Who knows how many more contributions of Blacks, both in Africa and diaspora, have gone unrecognized because of their colour. It is left to be imagined until some day.

But before you imagine too far, note that Dr. Charles Drew, a Black physician (African in diaspora) invented the process by which blood plasma is stored for later use. "Coming as it did on the eve of this country's entry into World War II," wrote Dewayne Wickham, a Minority Affairs columnist for Gannet News Service, "Drew's discovery saved the lives of hundreds of thousands of American GI's." Equally, a black doctor was the first to perform heart by-pass surgery. And successfully too.

As we go into the 1990's, some African-Americans are inevitably getting recognition in their respective professional careers, particularly if their achievements attain undeniable international acclaim.

Said Parade Magazine of December 25, 1988 about another Black (African-American or African in diaspora) medical doctor known as Dr. Benjamin Carson: The TV cameras had gone, and Benjamin Carson, M. D., was off the world's front pages, at least temporarily. The media long ago decided that this understated, hospitable young man was a miracle worker. First, he performed a rare brain operation that saved the life of a hydrocephalic baby still in the womb. Then, last year (in 1987), he was part of a team that separated siamese twins (flown from West Germany), born joined at the skull and sharing major blood systems to the brain, and left each one alive and intact."

Dr. Carson, 36 at this writing, was the Director of Pediatric Neurosurgery at the Johns Hopkins Children's Center. A graduate from Yale University, he has won two of the most prestigious awards in surgery and is considered a legend in his field. The Detroit (Michigan)-born Carson helped develop the surgical procedure used in the 22-hour operation/separation of Benjamin and Patrick Binder of West Germany who turned two years old in February 1989.

According to Michael Ryan who featured Dr. Carson in the Parade Magazine, "The operation took 22 hours, and for 14 of them Carson worked as a leading member of the 70-person team-- some of whom were doctors senior to him."

Did Benjamin Carson ever encounter any obstacles as he pioneered his medical profession? As a Black man, you bet he did. He described it this way: "The big difference between people who succeed and people who don't is not that the ones who are successful don't have barriers and obstacles. Everybody has barriers and obstacles. If you look at them as containing fences that don't allow you to advance, then you're going to be a failure. If you look at them as hurdles that strengthen you each time you go over one, then you're going to be a success," he emphasized.

Although Dr. Benjamin Carson is considered (as) a medical marvel, he is described as probably the only great surgeon without an ego to march because of his simplicity to life and living. It is still believed in some quarters that he got the undeniable media attention because his work had an unavoidable international acclaim. Otherwise, he could have been treated like others before him. Such as his namesake, Benjamin Banneker who made the first watch ever used in America, but was never recognized by the media, which his Black race did not and still does not have any major control or strong influence.

Let the West and its media debunk their bias and give Africa the respect it deserves. The truth of anyone's achievements, nations included, cannot be swept under the rugs forever. The truth must surface some day when the dust settles. May be it has started to settle for Africa and her diaspora.

* * *

EXOGENOUS USE OF AFRICANS

Africans have been exogenously used in countless times to undermine the exemplary work of their government and leaders. Most outstanding leaders of Africa with good intentions had been shamelessly assassinated in several occasions. This ranges from a giant nation like Nigeria to smaller ones like Seychelles.

Said African Concord Magazine of March 22, 1988, "The Democratic Republic of Sao Tome and Principe got a political jolt last week with a coup attempt said to have been masterminded by the Lisbon-based National Resistance Front . . . Government spokesman claimed that the Lisbon (Portugal) based group is on the payroll of the United States' Central Intelligence Agency and the secret service of racist South Africa."

Sao Tome and Principe, a tiny country with a population of about 100,000 people gained independence from the Portuguese on July 17, 1975. Since independence, it had practiced socialist system of government. That, perhaps, irks the American C. I. A.

Imagine what is happening in Mozambique and Angola. It is reminiscence of foreign orchestration. Mozambique has been in a civil war since its independence from Portugal on June 25, 1975. Encouraged by outside forces, rebels known as Renamo, now led by Afonso Dhlakama, 36, had been fighting the legitimate government, destabilizing and maiming innocent citizens, and destroying and damaging the economic and business outlays of the country.

Said American Newsweek magazine of February 1, 1988, "As many as 6.5 million Mozambicans could face starvation as a result of drought and the depredations of the rebels known as the Mozambique National Resistance or Renamo, whose support comes from right-wing sources in South Africa and the U.S.A. Determined to oust the Marxist-oriented Frelimo Government in Maputo (the capital), Renamo has cut rail lines, sacked villages and destroyed countless schools and clinics since it began intensifying its attacks in 1981. In a particular vicious assault in the town of Homoine last year," continued the magazine, "the rebels massacred nearly 400 civilians."

A U.S.A. ambassador to Mozambique, Melissa Wells, who personally is against the rebels incursion but whose country aids the rebels through the CIA, vented that "The destruction is maniacal."

Now one can imagine where Mozambique is going from here. According to the same Newsweek account, "Together with the outlaws, the rebels have driven more than one million people from their homes and halted food production by an estimated two million farmers. Once uprooted, the farmers are reluctant to plant again."

How then can the Frelimo government of President Joaquim Chissano who replaced Samora Machel who died in an air crash on October 19, 1986 near the border of South Africa, handle this fragile nation. Some Africans still share the view that South Africa shot down the Presidential jet with Machel and 34 others on board, as President Machel, who was unconditionally against apartheid, was returning from the just concluded Front Line States meeting held in Lusaka, Zambia. South Africa denied the accusation. Preliminary investigation was inconclusive.

The Angolan problem with South Africa has been since November 11, 1975 when it achieved its independence from Portugal. The white racist government of South Africa saw the Angolan attainment of independence as a threat to their continued illegal occupation of Namibia.

The South African government, through military invasion, raided the newly independent republic. Each of the attempts was thwarted by the Angolan forces. The racist regime continued its attempts from the independence day till 1976. It, however, resumed bombing and raiding of the Angolan south in 1978. This time, there was no relent on its dubious aggression. Initially, the Pretoria government claimed that the attack was justified by "hot pursuit" because of the alleged soldiers of South-West African People's Organization (SWAPO) -- the Namibian freedom fighters for Namibian independence from that pejorative South Africa -- which had bases in southern Angola. The Angolan President Jose Eduardo dos Santos was not amused.

This argument seemed credible until the aggression became clearly aimed at destroying purely Angolan targets and interests, such as schools, hospitals, communications and small towns like Ngiva.

This situation was aggravated by the use of mercenaries and guerrilla activities of Uniao Nacional Para a Independencia Total de Angola (UNITA), led by Jonas Savimbi. Dr. Savimbi who initially relied on the Portuguese armed forces for his insurgency before the independence of 1975, shifted his alliance to the apartheid South African regime. The Savimbi rebels were also financed by the United States, which out of innuendo with South Africa, is arguing against the presence of Cuban troops in the soil of Angola. Savimbi, a mere American and South African destructive tool, had in several occasions met with President Ronald Reagan (as a prospective head of state too?) in the White House, including the one they met on June 30, 1988. Reagan, as usual, promised further cooperation and financial assistance to their destabilization work.

The Cuban troops were in Angola (not for free though) to help her curtail, and in some cases forestall the incessant, imminent and unprovoked invasion of the country by the treacherous apartheid government of South Africa. Savimbi, whose personal ambition is to head or rule his country, would prefer the destabilization of his people to seeing the young nation succeed under the legitimate regime. He is continually and shamelessly financed by the Pretoria regime with impunity.

In the face of this posture, the racist regime starkly denies its Black citizens who form about 80% of the population, the basic human rights and enfranchisement. With bewilderment, one wonders where the conscience of Savimbi and any moral leadership lie. He most probably has a legitimate reason. But what bars him from cooperating with the government of his own country and bring changes from within, instead of betraying his persona by dining with the "enemy mine" -- the South African government. This is ludicrous and despicable, not only to his uninformed followers, but to the free-minded African thinkers and mankind. Without gain saying, one is left to imagine the kind of leader Savimbi would be if given the chance. Perhaps sell or give Angola back to the Portuguese. This is completely contrary to the cause Dr. Sam Nujoma, the SWAPO leader, is fighting for -- to liberate Namibia from South Africa.

But in fairness to Savimbi, the Frelimo government has its own blame. It seems to uncompromise on its philosophy of socialism. The government reneged its prerogative ingenuity of offering Jonas Savimbi some inducement he could not refuse, such as a cabinet position. Absolute rigidity does not work in these modern times. Guarded flexibility on either side is the key. A key to a win-win situation.

In its continuous use of Africans, CIA is shipping weapons to Savimbi through Zaire, whose leader, Mobutu Sese Seko, it helped to retain in power. To ship such arms through South Africa would violate the international arms embargo against apartheid South Africa.

Although one-party state does not give credence to accountability as well as reliable checks and balances, Dr.

Joshua Nkomo's eventual reconciliation with his arch political foe, Robert Mugabe, who excoriated and "chastised him with scorpion" since independence as he (Mugabe) was at the helm of Prime Ministership, is worth recognizing.

Having been an unsuccessful opposition leader for over 7 years, ostensibly due to his relatively minority tribe irrespective of being venerated within the continent as the father of Zimbabwe's nationalism, Nkomo signed unity accord with Mugabe on December 22, 1987. This accord, regarded in some quarters as fragile and vulnerable, would for now help Nkomo's Matabeleland people who had been treated with contempt since the attainment of independence.

In the new accord that automatically merged Nkomo's Zimbabwe African People's Union (ZAPU) to the ruling Zimbabwe African National Union (ZANU), Nkomo became one of the country's two vice-presidents, second secretary of the consolidated party, and Senior Minister in the President's office. Robert Mugabe, the former Prime Minister who solicited the deal, became the executive President. He equally retained defence portfolio. He was inaugurated on December 31, 1987.

To make the accord both credible and acceptable to the people of Matabeleland where Joshua Nkomo unquestionably gets his unalloyed political support, Mugabe rewarded Nkomo's two close lieutenants, John Nkomo (no relation to Joshua) and Joseph Msika with ministerial posts. John Nkomo was appointed the Minister of Labour, Manpower, Planning and Social Welfare, while Msika was given the Construction and National Housing post. Some other key positions, nonetheless, went to Mugabe's political allies. His deputy Prime Minister in the discarded republic, Simon Muzemba, shared the same rank, one of the vice-presidential posts, with Joshua Nkomo.

The compromise that Nkomo reached with Mugabe, though it might seem cowardly to an outsider, is an exemplary political attitude that other African opposition or minority leaders must emulate. There is an Igbo adage that says "Half [loaf of] bread is better than none." It takes courage, steadfastness, and serenity to accept defeat or give in to rivals, especially after every reasonable options had been exhausted.

From an objective evaluation point, Nkomo's compromise was not only fair and salvaging to his Matabeleland and nation, it was to give peace a chance. In addition to being a clear vindication that politics is the art of the possible, it equally showed an act of statesmanship on the part of Nkomo.

Jonas Savimbi of UNITA, Afonso

Dhlakama of Renamo rebels in Mozambique, and other disenchanted opposition thugs whose personal ambition and aggrandisement cloud their reasonable sense of judgment and every decency of civility, should learn how to swallow their pride and face the reality. For them to demolish with impunity and without any reasonable and foreseeable remorse, the existing infrastructure in their impoverished countries, subjugate their citizenry to utter helplessness, servitude and starvation through the financial and immoral support of exogenous elements that have high degree of tendentiousness toward their entire race, is not only idiotic and melancholic, it is abominable to say the least.

There is hope that it will come to pass when a wrong doer that is prone to pejorative attitude will repent. For the lasting interest of Africa, all Blacks should symbiotically work together for the common goal of their racial existence and progress. It is believed that justice will come when it will come. Even the most obscure fool or skeptic in South Africa, or perhaps the world, knows that changes will come in that morale beleaguered country that will benevolently affect the tantalized and touted Front Line states, perhaps including Nigeria that was symbolically admitted in mid-1988 at its request.

According to the Washington Post of August 4, 1988, "At a clandestine news conference in four South African cities, 143 men announced Wednesday (August 3, 1988) that they will refuse military service because it upholds the apartheid system of racial separation."

The paper estimated that "It was the largest expression of defiance of military call-ups to be conducted in South Africa's small but growing campaign to draft resistance by white youths. If they hold to their pledges, 105 of them face a mandatory six years' imprisonment. The others, who have served compulsory terms in the armed services, said they won't report for duty in summer reserve camps. They face prison terms of as long as three years."

Steven Silver, 22, a psychology student, was quoted as saying that he was willing to risk six years' imprisonment because the military "serves to prop up an unjust system of minority rule.

"Its role in the (Black) townships and my understanding of its destabilizing activity in the Southern African region forces me to reject it as having any possibility of adding to a peaceful solution to our country's problems," he said.

The protesters' inspiration came from the sentencing two weeks earlier of

David Bruce, 24, a student, who, out of political and moral grounds, was the first person to be given the six-year prison sentence for refusing to partake in the military service.

Margaret Thatcher, the Prime Minister of Britain, who has been an ardent supporter of South Africa and staunch opposer to economic sanctions to this repugnant regime, acknowledged this lurking and obvious realism recently.

To the astonishment of both her friends and foes, Mrs. Thatcher described apartheid as "repulsive, detestable and a deep affront to human dignity," before President Ibrahim Babangida, during her one day official (but not admired) visit to Nigeria on January 7, 1988. (President Babangida did not waste his time to welcome an apartheid sympathizer at the airport; a lower ranking official, amid an uncontrollable ocean of protesters, was sent.) In affirmation to what is starkly obvious, she emphasized, "Mr. President, change in South Africa will not be quick. But it must come. And it will come."

The menacing questions now are, how soon? and when? Perhaps when a brother starts being the brother's keeper, instead of the brother's killer. This, to a certain degree, will eliminate, if not exterminate, the exogenous political infringement into the African internal affairs.

Luckily, the change is underway. In early July 1988, the governments of Angola, Cuba, and South Africa agreed in principle to an accord through the auspices of the U. S. State Department led by the Assistant Secretary of State (for African Affairs) Chester Crocker, that would necessitate the eventual independence of Namibia.

The fragile accord, when implemented, assuming it would ever be, would involve the reduction of Cuban troops in Angola, the disbandment of UNITA guerrilla and infusion of its leaders into the ruling government functionaries. On their part, South Africa will accept and observe the United Nations' resolution 435 of 1978 mandating a de facto independence of Namibia, otherwise known as South-West Africa. The development has made the SWAPO leader, Dr. Sam Nujoma, more optimistic than ever, but with caution.

The future of the Namibian independence seems to be taking shape. According to the Los Angeles Times of August 9, 1988, "South Africa, Angola and Cuba, taking their first concrete step toward peace in Southwestern Africa, declared an immediate cease-fire Monday (August 8, 1988) in the 13-year-old Angolan civil war, and Pretoria (capital of South Africa) pledged to begin withdrawing its troops there by Wednesday (August 10, 1988)." South Africa completed its troop withdrawal from Angola on September 1, 1988.

"In the wake of their fourth round of peace talks last week in Geneva, the countries also agreed to ask the United Nations to implement, beginning November 1, 1989, the long-delayed plan for independence in Namibia, the mineral-rich territory that South Africa has ruled for 73 years. Firm agreement on Namibian independence still depends on overcoming one of the more difficult hurdles in the U. S. -mediated peace talks -- drawing up a timetable for withdrawal of the 50,000 Cuban troops helping Angola's government fight a rebel group supported by the United States and South Africa . . ." Luckily though, an agreement has been reached on that. In fact, Cuban troops' withdrawal started January 11, 1989.

The South African Foreign Minister, Roelof "Pik" Botha (no relation to President Pieter W. Botha) said in Pretoria that "This is the first step on a very long and arduous road to stability in the very important region of Southwestern Africa."

On the same Monday, August 8, 1988, their President, Pieter W. Botha, invited the U. N. Secretary-General Javier Perez de Cuellar to South Africa for discussions on the Namibian independence.

This probably was a mere public relations gesture, although there has been certain credibility to it since the treaties were signed December 22, 1988.

Nobody can precisely predict when this will completely come to fruition, especially as the South African Foreign Minister Botha, repeated his government's position that Namibian independence "is linked very clearly and categorically to the staged and total withdrawal of Cuban forces from Angola," and his government's belief that closing African National Congress (ANC) bases in Angola was a condition for peace in the region. In addition to ANC, what of the fate and role of UNITA and Southwest African People's Organization (SWAPO) -- the main Namibian guerrilla which had been fighting for independence in Namibia for 23 years?

If peace actually finds its good feet in the region as many have hoped-- except that one cannot trust the South African government -- then it is a milestone to really dissolving the exogenous destruction of Africa and dismantling of the "deep affront," as Mrs. Thatcher described apartheid in South Africa.

It is unquestionable that symbiotically and synergistically Africans can surmount all odds and any obstacles, and advance beyond imagination.

But again, this rests with the Africans. And everybody counts in such a struggle for African unity, coexistence, and economic and political advancement. Above all, we must learn to recognize our true friends and disguised enemies.

* * *

EDUCATION AND DEVELOPMENT

Said Diogenes, a Greek philosopher 412-323 B.C., *"The foundation of every state is the education of its youths."*

The importance of pragmatic education to the national building of any country cannot be over-emphasized. The problem of Africa in this case is that most people see education as an end itself, instead of an embryonic step, which is tantamount to beginning of the beginning to the tasks ahead.

Ideally, secondary school level should be the barest minimum educational standard any nation should mandatorily ask her citizens to attend. At that level, one can at least read, write, and most probably have a considerable ability to discern facts objectively. By the time one reaches this stage, one has probably reached a reasonable intellect to decide what one wants to do in life-- to continue the educational pursuit, or to assume family and the corresponding national responsibilities.

Most of the burden for the education of the youth, at least up to this secondary school level, should be carried by the state or nation. Even the United States of America, the symbol of the capitalist world, has free education to all and free lunch for destitute children from disadvantaged families up to high school level. This is necessary because the importance and value of education lasts forever, and the spillover effect is immeasurable.

From its editorial suite, Newswatch, a Nigerian weekly magazine of January 18, 1988 stated, "Education is the only solid foundation for a nation's progress. Its problems can be ignored at a great cost to the future of any nation."

Without education of the citizens, how can a nation handle its affairs, how much more of advancing scientifically and technologically.

But materialism is gradually taking a toll on the human mind. Wrote Dan Agbese of Newswatch of the same issue, "The children are not to blame. Man has never been able to solve himself as a problem. Man's best age is also the worst for his mind. His mind is cluttered with junk because the age of scientific and technological progress is the age of servitude -- servitude to materialism. It is the age of the neglect of the human mind -- that fine architecture of human thoughts . . ."

In a society where mind is less

refined, what happens? Continued Agbese, whose writings reflect the conscience of many, "The result is unprecedented savagery. Killing becomes a casual thing --something akin to a stroll in the moonlight. Violence is given recognition as a sociological right to protest injustice or draw attention to oneself. Vandalism is excused in the youth as adolescent right; it is excused in the old as an outlet for bottled frustration of growing old . . . But the laws of materialism do not recognize the human mind as the repository of human wisdom and not the storage tank for the dextritus of science and technology. The poor returns for handsome investments in the progress of man is nature's silent way of protesting the criminal neglect of the human mind." Then, "we are in bad trouble," he warned.

Education helps one to understand and discern facts before action follows. The gun shots from the stroke of a pen most of the time are more effective than from the real thing. Without well orchestrated education, could the late Rev. (Dr.) Martin Luther King, Jr. have, with tenacity and courage, carried out with much eloquency and ferocity his civil rights crusade of non-violence of the 1960s. He let himself undergo the rigorous educational training, up to doctoral level, before answering his full call for religious ministerial work which later transformed America.

It takes strength, sacrifice, and, of course, a high degree of discipline to undergo educational process. But at the end, the pride of academic sophistication, having the ability to distinguish facts from fiction, propaganda from truth, and the resultant improvement of quality of life through technological advancement and scientific research, override all the encumbrances and hassles.

Embarking on academic pursuit definitely causes postponed gratification. And it is only through dedication and well calculated discipline that all these can be achieved.

An example of such postponed gratification, dedication and discipline to acquire education, as exhibited by many African students studying in the United States of America and other foreign countries, can be found on the steadfastness, aggressiveness and tenacity of Stanley Akujor who hails from Inyishi in Mbaitoli/Ikeduru Local Government Area, Imo State, Nigeria. In fact, it was a tale that deserves a book of its own.

Although this author has never met Stanley in person at the time of this writing, he has, however, talked to him in numerous occasions in connection with his financial predicament while still pursuing his higher education.

Stanley came to the United States of America to attend Benedict College in South Carolina in January 1983. He graduated with the Highest Hono(u)rs two and a half years later. He left for Atlanta University where he was accepted for graduate studies in Political Science. He was, as a matter of fact, given a tuition only scholarship up to a Ph. D. level. But his eyes were set on law studies as his father, a local chief, had demanded.

He took the stringent LSAT exam (Law School Aptitude Test), applied for admission at several law schools and received three positive replies (admissions). Out of the three, he chose Thurgood Marshal School of Law at Texas Southern University in Houston, Texas, ostensibly due to the relatively low school fees. With only about $900.00 and his 1970 model Volkswagen Beetle which accommodated his scanty property, he headed for Houston, Texas in August 1987.

As he reached Houston to enroll for classes, he found out that without money or strong financial backing, educational advancement becomes very difficult and frustrating, especially in the study of law in the United States. With the help of the school Dean (Professor Carrington) whom he communicated his problems, he was allowed to enroll for 1987/88 school year with little or no money. The Dean's signature helped.

The policy of the school for an enrollment into the following semester (spring) was that a student must clear all his existing debt first. And without completing the full year, no credit is earned. But Stanley did not have the means. Again, in that spring semester that started in January 1988, his Dean who found him religious, brilliant, and trustworthy, came to the rescue. He "smuggled" him through the enrollment bureaucracy. And Stanley, who was very gratified, studied harder under hardship of no money for food or shelter. He slept in his car during most of the winter of 1988.

Luckily for him, out of about 200 first year law students that started together, he was among the 90 students that made it in grades. But at this time, his financial debt to the school had soured to about $4,250.00. And no means of payment was in sight. He was as poor as a church mouse.

Even being ordained as reverend and preacher of his protestant church back in South Carolina could not help him raise funds. Money was no more coming from home as it used to because of his country's voluntary devaluation of its currency (Naira) through the combination of the so-called second tier and

Structural Adjustment Programme (SAP) by more than 450%. The devaluation could not help his people raise an amount of his debt's magnitude, how much more of additional $5,000.00 (food and shelter not included) for the upcoming academic year tuition.

A strong condition set by the school for coming back for second-year status was to clear his debt. Still he persevered. But this time, neither he, nor the Dean could manipulate any loophole in the system. Stanley could not get any financial aid or educational loan because he had not changed his status to an American Immigrant resident. He looked for a job under the status of a student but couldn't get a decent one during the summer holiday preceding the 1988/89 school year. However, he got a mean job he was paid $20.00 a day for working 10 hours, even though a minimum wage set by law was $3.35 per hour. Well, he had no choice.

With no money to go back to school, no imminent help forthcoming from the helpful Dean Carrington, he had to forgo going to school for the 1988/89 school year.

Even his American acquaintance who cajoled him since two years earlier to the point of marriage commitment, deserted him too, on the ground that he put education first before her. Stanley was left in the cold. This was a very temptable and trying period. He was not only thinking of what to eat, where to sleep, or the education that has nearly reached the dead end, but about the Immigration and Naturalization Service which could haunt him as soon as it learned that he has lost his student "status."

Now, thanks to certain amnesty provisions in the amendment to U.S. Immigration law that ended in late 1988, Stanley is now safe.

With limited options left, he took a one year leave of absence from his law school to see if he can regroup, then make a comeback (later) to face his old debt, and perhaps the accumulating ones.

At about age 29 by 1989, the perseverance and struggle for the Doctor of Jurisprudence (J.D.) for Rev. Stanley Akujor continued. His dream for now is education and not wealth. And some people might now ask, why?

The "why?" question may be answered from what Adam Smith in 1776 wrote in his book, The Wealth of Nations. Said he, "A man educated at the expense of much labour and time to any one of those employments which require extraordinary dexterity and skill may be compared to one of those expensive machines." Perhaps this statement makes sense to the subject at hand only by implication, or by considering the sacrifice endured by the student and the financial investment of his parents, friends and loved ones.

The quest for world materialism has thwarted African mentality and morality. People now drop out of school permanently in search of mystified wealth. Those who manage to complete their education, while competing for materialistic achievement to maintain their egoistic hedonism, unfortunately indulge in the malpractice of bribery and corruption. Some have adopted a consoling slogan of "If you can't beat them, join them." The eventual results, invariably are inefficiency and degeneration of services at the expense and marred reputation of the respective nations in particular, and Africa in general.

Government services are the most wanting in Africa. Most government workers, irrespective of their level of education, fail to understand that the government they serve is theirs. A worker is supposed to have a patriotic part to play for the smooth running of his government. Unfortunately, the patriotism is virtually lacking in Africa today. This lackadaisical attitude, with its perplexity, is drifting into the commercial sector. What a sorry situation.

Wrote Bayo Onanuga of African

Concord Magazine of February 2, 1988, on how the disdainful attitude to the government function by the civil servants came about in Africa: " . . . That was Nigeria's bureaucracy at birth in 1862, as an imperial tool, anchored on imperial motives, used for imperial ends. Its initial staffers were Britons, and educated natives, recruited on equal pay until 1890 when Governor Carter introduced a policy of white supremacy. White workers did the same job with natives but they went home with differentiated wages. The locals were infuriated, alienated. The alienation became a credo for the Nigerian workers and the public they served. No one wanted to identify with the civil service, no one saw it as serving his interests, no one wished its prosperity. No one cared if it failed. That patent indifference became a religion with swelling adherents that survived 27 (Nigeria had her political independence on October 1, 1960) years of Nigeria's independence."

Corruption and indifference by workers are much worse at the government parastatals and agencies. Some employees of the government owned Nigerian External Telecommunications (NET) or Nigerian Telecommunications Limited (NITEL) are on the payroll of some Nigerian businessmen in order to augment their poor income. In return, any calls made by these business tycoons are put in other persons or companies' bill. If any of those persons or companies dispute the calls, their telephone lines are almost always cut off. Most of the time the only option left in order to get out of it is to bribe those unscrupulous employees for them to remove those calls, perhaps to other persons or companies' bills.

No one cares to listen without bribe; not even their bosses. There is usually no good business spirit. It is believed that Col. David Mark, under Gen. Babangida Administration, tried hard to correct the odious and archaic system without much success.

Thus, the cycle of inefficiency, corruption and bribery continues. After all, it is not their fathers' company. It is a government owned corporation -- a no man's concern.

This is a reflection of what is going on in most African countries today. But then, why commercial sector too?

Education, no doubt, helps people to modify their ways. It is mostly through education that one will be willing to see the other side of oneself. It also helps people to adjust to this fast changing world quicker and still be able to recognize the variation in human creatures.

Man is naturally wicked and envious.

Man always wants things to go his way. He rebuffs criticism. He likes to uproot any obstacles or those considered as inhibition to his own "progress." Everyone wants to win. But it is often forgotten that one cannot triumph all the time. As such, one must always have the courage to belly defeat.

Certainly, it is mostly through education, reeducation, and retraining that man changes his old ways. Everyone has some degree of innate ability. It is developed, enhanced, shaped and sharpened through continuous learning. Through objective subjugation to learning, one is poised to see from one's mind's eye that things are not merely black or white, but are made up of separate points on a continuum with other colours in between.

Nze Wilfred Onyeadusi Nwachukwu, once told this author at his tender-age that education, though very necessary, does not produce wisdom alone. He stressed that wisdom mostly comes from erudition coupled with experience. This, ironically, has some elements of validity. Education merely facilitates understanding, which, of course, leads to experience, hence wisdom.

One needs to open one's mind in order to acquire learning. Said a special advertisement in the United States of America by the United Negro College Fund -- an organization that solicits and helps to fund most Black universities and colleges -- "A mind is a terrible thing to waste."

Even Malcolm X (birth given name was Malcolm Little), a Black civil rights activist and an advocate for violence against white Americans at the height of overt racism in the United States of America in the 1950s and '60s, gave encouraging words for education. Said he, "Education is an important element in the struggle for human rights. It is the means to help our children and our people rediscover their identity and thereby increase self-respect. Education is our only passport to the future, for tomorrow belongs only to the people who prepare for it today."

Dr. William Cosby, popularly known in the entertainment world simply as Bill Cosby of The Cosby Show, echoed the same thing about the education of Black Americans in his special appearance at the Tony Brown Journal showed on Public Television station, Channel 13, in Dallas, on Tuesday, April 26, 1988. He said that education was a "passport" for decent life for Blacks in America. One with education would have respect, he said. He would not mug an old woman to snatch $5.00 from her purse. Cosby himself has a doctoral degree. He pursued education while still acting in the entertainment business.

Not changing with time has been the major setback for Africa. In some cases, unwarranted schism and tribal melancholy disrupt developmental projects. One becomes ashamed of one's country, continent and the beleaguered people. Instead of upward bound, it becomes retrogression. Even the countries nowadays fail to retain their educated people because of political skirmishes.

Why can't Africa have a breakthrough in sciences and technology? Perhaps in some cases they do than are given credit for. But there are more brain drain of Africans today than in the past because of political instability in most of the regions. The iconoclasts are hardly given the chance to voice their opinion. Their reaction most of the time is a quiet exodus to other political and economic stable nations.

On December 29, 1987, a Soviet cosmonaut named Yuri Romanenko, who spent 326 days in space, descended to the earth. What a remarkable achievement. But more exuberating was the fact that two fellow cosmonauts, Vladimir Titov and Musa Manarov returned to earth on Wednesday, December 21, 1988, after making history's longest space flight in orbit. Their Soyuz TM-6 capsule parachuted safely to Soviet Central Asia at 12:57 p.m. Moscow time. The Soviets blasted off at 2:18 p.m. December 21, 1987, according to the (U.S.) Associated

Press.

The flight by Titov and Manarov lasted 365 days, 22 hours and 39 minutes; thus, breaking the 326-day mark set by Yuri Romanenko a year earlier. The longest manned mission by U. S. astronauts -- Gerald Carr, Edward Gibson and William Pogue -- aboard the Skylab Space Station lasted only 84 days. That happened in 1973.

It is now believed that the mission by Titov and Manarov has given the Soviets a valuable experience as they prepare for a three-year journey to the planet Mars. Soviet officials have indicated that a manned mission to Mars will be launched about the turn of the century. It must be mentioned here that in space, man does not have weight. He regains his weight as he descends to this earth of high gravity.

In the same world of science, J. Robert Oppenheimer, formerly Director of Los Alamo National Laboratory based in New Mexico state in the U. S. A., who died in 1967, was known as the father of the atomic bomb. Dr. Edward Teller, 81 at this writing, who was in charge of the Lawrence Livermore National Laboratory in California, is known as the father of the hydrogen bomb. Albert Einstein won the Nobel Prize in physics in 1921 for discovering the law of the photoelectric effect. At present, America has three laboratories where research in nuclear weapons' design is operational: the two mentioned above and Sandia National Laboratory, also in New Mexico. And Israel, on September 19, 1988, sent its own satellite into orbit (by its technology.)

Now, where is Africa? A continent for that matter!! Israel, South Africa, and Pakistan, whose nuclear and atomic bomb capabilities have reached production level, need not be mentioned. How come African nations can't genuinely compete in a scientific and technological sphere, instead of mere political and wasteful internal struggle. Nigeria, like Libya, is rumoured to have reached the production level of atomic/nuclear bomb, but this could not be confirmed in Nigeria because of her official secrecy act.

The quest to learn, at least up to secondary school level, either free or heavily subsidized by the state, should be a right rather than a privilege. Everyone gains out of this because of the spill-over effect. Most of the nationalists who fought for and gained the independence of these nations had to go through the regiment and concocted discipline of this cult called education.

With that acquired knowledge, they were equipped for the forthcoming challenges of being the master of their own fate. You see some of the wonders of education? But today, are we ready for tomorrow?

Tanzania is now leading in the literacy rate in Africa, and probably in the world, with her literacy rate at 90.4% in 1988. By the 1990s, the government targets 96%. How did this happen?

The campaign to wipe out illiteracy in Tanzania started in 1970, according to the African Concord of May 17, 1988. In 1971, the government of Dr. Julius Nyerere declared its intention to wipe out illiteracy within five years. "With about 70 per cent of its population illiterate and its poor economy, the mission seemed unattainable," said the paper.

"By the end of 1975, the target had not been met. But over 5,000,000 Tanzanians had enrolled in adult classes and illiteracy was down from 70% to about 40%. By 1977 it had fallen to 27% and by 1981 to 21%," the paper said.

This achievement was indeed remarkable. UNESCO heralded it as the steepest sustained fall in illiteracy ever achieved by any nation.

By the time Dr. Nyerere left office in 1985, the literacy rate had significantly jumped to 85%; thus, the illiteracy rate was down to 15%. By 1988, the literacy rate had reached 90.4%, steeping illiteracy further to about 9%.

Why was this possible? The African Concord had an answer: The political commitment of the nation's leadership-- a commitment arising from the belief that the development of 'human resources' is both the end and means of development itself.

While launching the campaign for literacy in 1970, Dr. Julius K. Nyerere, in a form reminiscent of philosophizing, said, "First we must educate our adults. Our children will not have an impact on our economic development for five, ten or twenty years. The attitudes of the adults, on the other hand, have an impact now." Think about it. While the youth or children are our future, the adults lead now. And most of the time, children emulate or acquire the traits of the adults. As such, both should be educated in their various ways somewhat simultaneously.

In order to maintain and eventually advance beyond their projected points, Africans must learn and work relentlessly, and harder too. No time to waste.

Life is never easy. There are many rivers to cross, including River Rubicon, before one gets to manhood. The same applies to nations. But the foundation must be concreted on a rock; otherwise, when the strong North-East trade wind, with all its intensity, blows, it uproots the shaky and fragile base to obscurity.

And that rock for any nation, the rock of ages, even if belated, is education in all its ramifications.

* * *

THE FUTURE OF AFRICA

The most difficult thing to predict is future, any psychical or astrological ability notwithstanding. Anything can happen in the long run. Economists simply say that in the long run, "everything" is variable.

It is rational to say that one determines one's destiny. That applies to countries, as well as continents and their inhabitants. As such, the fate of Africa is squarely on the hands of Africans. This leads one to see clearly that African problems today are mostly endogenous with a few exogenous factors. The bribery and corruption in Africa are caused by Africans. The inefficiency in the government and private sectors is the handiwork of Africans. Tribalism, nepotism, and embezzlement perpetrated in the society are mostly endogenous. Foreign infiltration, which is merely sporadic, simply exacerbate it.

This kind of situation forces one to lament thus: "Oh!! God protect me from my friends, for I will take care of my enemies." This stretches one's mind to

Shakespeare's Julius Caesar, in the fracas of Caesar and Brutus. Remember the famous lament of "Oh! Brutus, you too?" by Caesar, his last words before his final demise.

Foreign leaders simply use Africans for their political and economic ends. No two persons are absolutely alike, although they may be similar. As such, no two countries can follow strictly the political and economic philosophy of each other. This is due to different structural, economical and political backgrounds of the respective countries.

It is absolutely unfair to subjugate any nation or its leaders to perdition, excoriation or persecution because of political and economic variation from the West. Neither is it acceptable for the Communist world to do the same to any nation that is leaning towards capitalism. It is tantamount to complete idiotism to say the least, for any African to be a tool or destructive agent for the West or Eastern blocs against his own nation. Such dubious mentality and treachery must be exorcised to its very root in Africa. But it must be through civilized means and not through "ordeal."

The way the so-called Renamo, also known as Mozambique National Resistance (MNR) has been causing havoc, destroying the young nation's meagre infrastructure, and perpetrating mayhem on the innocent citizens are very despicable. Even Jonas Savimbi, a supposedly learned man, is among the ones that condescended to this low ebb. Getting lethal help from the enemies of his race -- impliedly against his very existence -- to destabilize his nation is reprehensible.

Assuming that he succeeds in dethroning the Luanda government, how can he rebuild the remnants of his destruction. Does he think that those who are ready to give him the destructive arms to kill or exterminate his brethren would generously give him the economic assistance of high magnitude to rebuild the demoralized and battered nation? And does he believe that if he takes over power that another insurgence against him would not arise. He should have borrowed a cue from other African countries. The optimum solution to the political polarization in his country is to be pragmatic. This means, negotiate in good faith, surrender (his) arms, and join the legitimate government for the common good of the people and country.

His refusal will be costly, not only to him but to his followers, especially as South Africa kept its promise of pulling out its insurgent troops from Angolan borders. It has even started to cost him dearly.

According to James Brooke of New York Times News Service, as reported by the Dallas Morning New of Sunday, October 9, 1988, "Angola's military has recaptured a string of rebel towns, including the birthplace of rebel leader Jonas Savimbi" since South Africa's troops pullout from Angola September 1, 1988. " . . .In the offensive for Savimbi's native village of Munhango," continued Brooke, "government troops confronted nine rebel battalions, killing 1,300 defenders, Angola's Chief of Military Intelligence, Lt. Col. Mario Placido Cirilo de Sa, said in an interview here Friday (October 7, 1988). The village fell September 13, 1988."

According to the government report, Savimbi's guerrillas lost 74 vehicles and 650 weapons, and 3,000 land mines were deactivated. The government casualties were put at 50 dead and 294 wounded.

James Brooke, in the same article, stated that "The Untied States, the rebels' other major supplier, is believed to ship weapons through Zaire. To send American weapons through South Africa," he reasoned, "would violate an international arms embargo of South Africa."

Although Zaire's officials deny allowing transshipments of arms to the rebels, Angolan President Jose Eduardo dos Santos insisted, most probably with good evidence, that "UNITA members and arms are continuing to cross the border from Zaire." Zaire shares a common border with Angola. This accusation makes much sense, especially as President Mobutu Sese Seko of Zaire dined with Pieter Botha, the racist President of South Africa, who paid him an official visit during the first week of October, 1988. Mobutu falsely claimed to have obtained the release of Nelson Mandela during his tete-a-tete discussion with Botha. The release never was, at least not as he claimed. He even promised to visit South Africa -- a land where black majority are barely treated as second class citizens, how much more as first class. A country where the citizenship of a person of Archbishop Desmond Tutu's stature "will be determined at a future date."

Based on the atrocities Savimbi and his followers committed, not only to Angolans but Black men in general, he can never be forgiven. And Angolans know that.

A good look at the entire Dallas Times Herald editorial of Thursday, October 13, 1988 titled "Angolan Peace a U.S. Success," can give one an independent understanding on what the U.S. and other powers have done and can do in Africa.

Said the maverick Dallas Times Herald, "Assistant Secretary of State Chester A. Crocker, through dogged determination and remarkable negotiating skill, appears close to forging a working settlement to both the 13-year-old Angolan civil war and the 21-year occupation of Namibia by South African troops.

"If final details can be ironed out, the Crocker formula would end big-power tensions in the region, prompt the withdrawal of 50,000 Cuban troops from Angola and thousands of South African troops from Namibia, bring independence to long-suffering Namibia and produce the first major success in the oft-criticized African policies of the Reagan administration.

"It is in everyone's interest that Mr. Crocker succeed, though it means ending American support for the Angolan rebel movement under Jonas Savimbi."

How was the American CIA involved with the Angolan conflict in the first place?

Continued the editorial, "The situation is complex. Angola was the last of the Portuguese colonies in Africa, and when it won its liberation in 1974, the CIA went looking for a faction to support.

"There were three primary revolutionary movements: UNITA, headed by Jonas Savimbi, supported by the Nuvumba tribe in the South; the MPLA, under Jose Eduardo dos Santos, comprised of Angola's largest tribe, the Mbundu; and the FNLA under Holden Roberto, made up of the Bakongo tribe in the North. The MPLA was funded by the Soviet Union, the others by the communist China."

How did UNITA all of a sudden become "Democratic freedom fighters?"

Continued the paper, "The CIA selected a group not supported by the Soviets, dubbed them democratic freedom fighters and provided $31.7 million in cash and arms to help them win control over the country. Messrs. Roberto and dos Santos made up, rather than engage in a destructive civil war.

"Mr. Savimbi, with the aid of the CIA, South Africa and disgruntled Portuguese business interests, has been fighting ever since. In recent years, they were often aided by South African troops stationed in Namibia, which has been occupied as a buffer state for two decades.

"The conflict resulted in Cuba sending troops to Angola in increasing numbers to help build a fledgling country, protect American oil companies in northern Angola, and repel the troops of Savimbi and its South African allies."

Was there ever any linkage between

the Namibian independence and Cuban presence in the land of sovereign Angola nation? The answer is absolutely, no.

Said the editorial, "Prior to the Reagan administration, Namibian independence and the Angolan turmoil were distinct issues. Mr. Crocker proposed linkage: Namibian freedom in exchange for a Cuban troop pullout.

"His approach has been criticized, but that is precisely the deal being struck. It was aided by Soviet President (formerly General-Secretary) Mikhail Gorbachev, who has made it clear to Cuba that he wants their foreign adventurism curtailed. With that imperative, Namibian independence became a viable negotiating pawn, as Mr. Crocker foresaw.

"A sticking point remains. The Reagan administration, bowing to conservative pressures at home, insists it can continue supplying arms and money to Mr. Savimbi's Chinese-trained 'freedom fighters,' which makes the Cubans uneasy about completely pulling out of the area. The Cubans are still arguing about the time table.

"If the overriding concern is to eliminate the Cuban presence and the influx of Soviet military material into Angola," continued this objective and frank editorial by the Dallas Times Herald, "then the United States should end its support for a destabilizing army, and leave Angola's future to Angolans."

Is there any paradox in American covert and overt destabilization of Angola through the use of UNITA? Of course, yes.

"It has long been paradoxical that Cuba should send its troops thousands of miles to use Soviet weapons to protect American oil workers from Angolan dissidents using weapons paid for by American taxpayers. Thanks to the redoubtable Mr. Crocker, all that adventurism should cease," concluded the swift and carefully worded editorial by this respectable giant newspaper in Dallas, Texas.

The lesson Africans and the world alike must learn is that one good turn deserves another, and a coup necessitates a counter-coup. Except in some isolated genuine occasions, greed, personal ambition or hunger for power causes most of Africa's problems. Imagine what happened in Burkina Faso, where Capt. Blaise Compaore and his loyalists assassinated and hurriedly buried in a mass grave the body and soul of an upright president like Capt. Thomas Sankara on October 15, 1987. He was so upright that he changed his nation from Upper Volta, a colonial name, to Burkina Faso, which in native languages means "Land of the upright men." Now the uprightness of his people is questionable. And how upright Capt. Compaore would be is left to be seen.

Under such circumstances, a counter-coup is foreseeable; if not in the short term, at least in the long run, because he (Compaore) lacked a good explanation and/or intention for dethroning and wilfully murdering such a rare honest figure. Political oppositions against him, particularly RDP-Thomas Sankara, have grown in size and clout despite all the vigilante effort by the security agents to victimize and exterminate them. Perhaps the ironical "good" efforts by the opposition would help make the lives of Sankara's wife, Mariam, his mother, Marguaritta, and children bearable.

Irrespective of all these shortcomings among Africans, the future looks bright. Africa has moved from the "darkness" without history, to a continent where man actually originated. From colonized to a virtually politically independent continent. The only bottleneck in the total liberation of Africa is the repugnant nonchalant attitude of the racist South African government against the Black majority citizens, and the illegal and imperialistic occupation of Namibia by the outrageous regime. But one day, South Africans shall be free. And one day, Namibia shall also be free, especially now that a meaningful and hopeful agreement has been reached, signed and sealed by the connected parties.

That United States' mediated peace accord between Angola and South Africa, with Cuba participating, was officially signed at the United Nations Organisation's Social and Economic Council Chamber in New York, at the presence of the U.N. Secretary General, Javier Perez de Cuellar, on Thursday, December 22, 1988. Representing their respective countries during the signing "ceremony" were foreign ministers George P. Shultz for the United States, Alfonso Dan Duneu for Angola, Isodoro Malmierca for Cuba, Roelof "Pik" Botha for the socially ostracized and racist South Africa, and Soviet Deputy Foreign Minister Anatoly Adamishin.

The first batch of Cuban withdrawals started on January 11, 1989 with mixed emotions on both sides of Cuba and Angola. The United Nations Organisation pledged to send several thousand peace-keeping forces or observers to monitor the progress from both Angola and South Africa and the total independence of Namibia which was the core issue of the accord. Angolans and Cubans are playing their parts effectively; who knows what South Africa has under its sleeves. But it will certainly face strong world condemnation if it reneges its agreed part, among other things, to give Namibia its overdue independence on April 1, 1990.

Even in Ethiopia, there are renewed hope and progress toward peace. On September 13, 1988, President Mengistu Haile Mariam, as a 14th anniversary gift of his socialist revolution, proposed a plan that would grant autonomy to five regions in Ethiopia, which under a constitutional provision or setting, would give them self-governing status but responsible to the president at the federal level. This kind of governmental plan is otherwise known as a confederation. He asked Ethiopians, both the rebels and the nation's armed forces, to join hands with him in such peace effort that would resolve the nearly quarter-of-a-century-old bloodshed there. Among the regions included in the autonomy proposal were the two war-torn provinces in the North and Southeast of the country -- Eritrea and Tigre (or Tigray) respectively -- as well as Ogaden, which for several years was a source of conflict between Ethiopia and Somalia, in addition to Assaba and Diredawa. Eritrea People's Liberation Front (EFLP) and the Tigray People's Liberation Front (TFLP) had for over two decades been fighting for separate independence.

If this new political formula is honestly followed by President (formerly Lt. Col.) Mariam and accepted by the warring parties, then the wind of peace which is gradually blowing across the

African continent, must have found its berth in this famine-devastated nation. At least their resources could be pooled together to improve the standard of living and quality of life of the people, instead of enriching the developed nations by patronizing their stock-piled destructive weapons.

Thus, the total liberation of Africa from all the vestiges of colonialism. The Namibian independence may come by April 1, 1990 (full independence) if the agreement mentioned earlier in this book, and signed at the United Nations Headquarters in New York, U.S.A., on December 22, 1988 is followed by the letters.

What Africa must gear toward now is economic revitalization and independence. As also mentioned earlier in this book, one who pays for the piper dictates the tune. And, of course, there is no free lunch.

The world is a stage of quid pro quo. If you have nothing to give, you receive nothing in return. But if you have a dream, a visionary dream and goes after it, you have the world to conquer. Even the Holy Bible somewhat agrees. In the parable of the Minas, Luke 19:26, it says, "For I say to you, that everyone who has will be given; and from him who does not have, even what he has will be taken away from him."

Africa has been pushed around too much and for too long. A continent with so much nations, human and natural resources, but no super-power or a permanent member of the United Nations Security Council. Imagine that. Europe has two -- Britain and France; Asia has two -- Soviet Union and China; North America has the United States of America. The "good" excuse Africans espouse is that their nations are relatively young. This is a sham excuse on the ground that most of their nations get economically and politically debased as they grow older, instead of striving or rejuvenating into vigour. This is paradoxical indeed.

When Africans eventually wake up from the trance, traumatism, and prolonged slumber, they will start to elect dedicated leaders to office, as opposed to tribesmen and gluttonous vote riggers and purchasers; they will start to think of community instead of individualism; protect their nation and continent as opposed to mere self; think in terms of aggregate as against units.

If the interest of the community, nation and continent is seriously put into consideration by Africans before any action, no matter how trivial, is taken, certain abhorrent and mischievous activities perpetrated by some of them probably would never happen. Most of the time, it is pragmatic, and perhaps more intelligible to reform from within than from outside political forum where one is considered a total stranger and enemy of progress, whether imagined or real. The initial frustration and inevitable distrust are understandable. But the ultimate result with persistence and maturity would be worth the effort.

It is quite perceivable that some people are locked out of the political process. This in most cases leads to a revolt. In such a condition, acting under an extenuating circumstance that may mitigate legal effects, it is permissible, if ever it is necessary, to carry out certain illegitimate actions to attract attention or redirect priorities. But one does not suppress issues and/or any government benevolent actions from their incipiency without exploring all the pertinent and implied infinitesimal ramifications. One does not be against the philosophy of one's government from day one of its independence simply because one's political party was not favoured by the electorates. This vicissitude amounts to selfishness and unnecessary credo.

Wake up ladies and gentlemen of Africa. Let peace and freedom get a chance. Let "uhuru" take its course. It is obvious that this optimism will eventually come to pass in Africa. One yearns to the day when African progress will be envied by the rest of the world, in terms of economic buoyancy, technological advancement, political tranquility, and moral behaviourism.

The posterity has a difficult job ahead. They will right today's political and economic mistakes, just like the nationalists of our time are righting the yester-year's injustice of the colonial exploitations and inflicted miseries. But an impeccable foundation in which the children will work from must be laid solid.

A lot of good economic planning, barring forceful and effective implementation, has started in Africa. Yakubu Gowon of Nigeria, before he was rightfully ousted from power on July 29, 1975, initiated the Economic Community for West African States (ECOWAS). This has its modality from the European Economic Community (EEC), commonly referred to as the Common Market of Europe. Although ECOWAS was not as vibrant as the EEC, it was a step in the right direction in the continent.

Other sub-African regions, such as the Front Line States in the Southern African Region, which among others include Botswana, Zambia, Zimbabwe, Mozambique, Tanzania, and Angola, have embarked in a similar economic cooperation within themselves. On the same vein, in 1976, Rwanda, Burundi, and

Zaire established the Economic Community of Great Lakes Countries. That was an enviable move toward economic cooperation.

The Organization of African Unity (OAU), founded on May 25, 1963 at a conference held in Addis Ababa, Ethiopia, which is also its permanent headquarters, is another important milestone used to unify and galvanize Africa.

The roads to a strong and unified Africa are rough, especially as its people are used against themselves. Hitherto, divided. But it is a turbulent weather that is sailable. It all hinges on Africans. If they can dream it, they can achieve it. But it equally requires a high dose of discipline, unputrefaction, persistence and untainted sacrifice.

It must be remembered that it is very easy to destroy than to build or rebuild. Even the biblical parable implies that too. As such, there must be hope left for the new generation and beyond. It is a task that must be done- a BRIGHT AFRICA.

But as Niccolo Machiavelli observed in 1514, and gracefully noted by this author in his first book titled, THE AGONY: The Untold Tale Of The Nigerian Society, transition, euphemically known as change, is difficult to be accepted initially. There must be some degree of resistance at some quarters. That is a raw human nature.

Said Machiavelli, "*It should be borne in mind that there is nothing more difficult to arrange, more doubtful of success, and more dangerous to carry through than initiating changes . . . The innovator makes enemies of all those who prospered under the old order, and only lukewarm support is forthcoming from those who would prosper under the new. Their support is lukewarm partly from fear of their adversaries, who have the existing laws on their side, and partly because men are generally incredulous, never really trusting new things unless they have tested them by experience.*"

Then how does one test something by experience under certain circumstances without embarking on it or trying the change and/or taking a chance.

These typically are what is going on in the world, particularly in Africa. Or isn't it? It has to be understood that the only thing to fear is fear itself. Note that trial is no failure. Not trying at all is.

When Africans were fighting for political freedom in the early 20th century, Dr. Kwame Nkrumah of Ghana said, "*Seek ye first the political kingdom and all things shall be added unto you.*"

That made sense then. But in the 21st century, the slogan has to change. It should be, seek first the economic and technological power, and everything else is at your whim. That is what the Japanese people have done recently and are still doing.

The wave of change continues without aberration. Any interference to the inevitable changes toward the BRIGHT AFRICA, will cause things to fall apart, and the centre may not hold any more . . . Hence, mere anarchy may be loosed upon the world . . . And some disgruntled and bewildered elements may start to ask, Oh Gosh!! Why? Why?

But had I known usually comes at last. As President John F. Kennedy of the United States of America said in his inaugural address of January 20, 1961 for his nation, Africans equally must be willing to pay any price, bear any burden, meet any hardship, support any friend, oppose any foe, to assure the survival and the success of liberty in African soil, in addition to political stability, technological advancement and economic progress -- thus, the much needed Bright Africa.

As Hughes, Meltzer, and Lincoln wrote in 1956, "The decline of Songhay and Timbuktu in the Seventeenth Century signaled the end of an epoch of the great civilizations of West Africa. But the glory of Africa, that most ancient of ancient lands, must not sleep for long. There is a biblical tradition which promises that 'Ethiopia shall stretch forth her wings.' The fortunes of Africa will be reversed. Her greatness," they emphasized, "will be restored."

There is a past which is gone forever. But there is a future which is still our own. And that future starts today, especially as an old adage says that every action of our lives, touches some chord that will vibrate to eternity. Now is your chance.

* * *

SPECIAL ACKNOWLEDGEMENT

1. Dallas Morning News, Texas (USA) October 3, 1985
2. Dallas Morning News, Dallas, Texas (USA) July 24, 1988
3. Dallas Times Herald, Dallas, Texas (USA) November 8, 1985
4. Dallas Times Herald, Dallas, Texas (USA) July 5, 1988
5. Dallas Times Herald, Dallas, Texas (USA) October 13, 1988
6. African Concord (Nigeria) February 2, 1988
7. African Concord (Nigeria) March 22, 1988
8. African Concord (Nigeria) May 16, 1988
9. Newswatch (Nigeria) November 23, 1987
10. Newswatch (Nigeria) December 21, 1987
11. Newswatch (Nigeria) January 18, 1988
12. News Week (USA) January 11, 1988
13. News Week (USA) February 1, 1988
14. News Week (USA) December 5, 1988
15. Los Angeles Times, August 9, 1988
16. Washington Post (USA) August 4, 1988
17. Africa South of Sahara, 1987 Edition

18. PERHAM, M. and J. SIMMONS, African Discovery: Anthology of Exploration, 1942
19. CURTIN, P. D., Image of Africa: British Ideas and Actions 1780-1850
20. HUGHES, LANGSTON, MILTON MELTZER, AND C. ERIC LINCOLN, A Pictorial History of Black Americans
21. DUBOIS, W. E. B., World and Africa
22. DAVIS, RONALD W., Negro Contribution to the Exploration of the Globe, p. 33
23. Keesing's Research Report 6: Africa Independent - A Study of Political Developments, Charles Scribner's Sons, New York, 1972
24. SAMKANGE, STANLAKE (The Professor sadly passed away in Zimbabwe in March 1988), African Saga - A Brief Introduction to African History, 1971
25. CHAMBERLAIN, M. E., The Scramble For Africa, Longman Group Ltd., 1974 and 1977
26. GUTTERIDGE, WILLIAM F., The Military In African Politics, Methuen & Co. Ltd., London, 1969
27. DAVIDSON, BASIL, Africa In History: Themes And Outlines
28. OLIVER, R., J. O. FAGE, A Short History of Africa, 1962
29. DAVIDSON, BASIL, Black Mother: The Years of the African Slave Trade
30. DAVIDSON, BASIL, Old Africa Rediscovered, 1959
31. CAIRNS, H. A. C., Prelude to

Imperialism: British Reactions to Central African Society, 1840-1890, Routledge, 1965
32. Parade Magazine (USA) December 25, 1988